# RESTORING GLORY

## SCOTT CUONG TRAN AND NICK TRAN

KEY
Books

### Dedication

For Sheila Yau

**FRONT COVER IMAGE:** What's better than one Mustang? Two Mustangs, of course! *Gunfighter* and *Charlotte's Chariot II* fly in formation, demonstrating the skill of their pilots.

**BACK COVER IMAGE:** Once mortal foes, *X-133* has joined up with a Corsair and a Hellcat to show that even the most bitter enemies can eventually become friends.

**TITLE PAGE IMAGE:** This rare formation includes Allied aircraft fighters led by a Mosquito.

**CONTENTS PAGE IMAGE:** Being on the business end of a diving Lightning would cause much consternation, as many Luftwaffe and Japanese pilots found out.

Published by Key Books
An imprint of Key Publishing Ltd
PO Box 100
Stamford
Lincs
PE19 1XQ

www.keypublishing.com

The rights of Scott Cuong Tran and Nick Tran to be identified as the authors of this book has been asserted in accordance with the Copyright, Designs and Patents Act 1988 Sections 77 and 78.

Typeset by SJmagic DESIGN SERVICES, India.

# CONTENTS

Avengers and Wildcats were able to inflict heavy damage on the Imperial Japanese Navy, with Avengers sinking ships and Wildcats shooting down enemy aircraft.

# INTRODUCTION

A massive paradigm shift occurred for military strategists with the introduction of armed aircraft. An additional warfighting domain was suddenly introduced, and generals were forced to consider the skies as an equal, if not more important, battlefield to the land and sea. Control of the air provides massive advantages, including strategic bombardment, close air support, intelligence gathering, and transport abilities. Famed airpower theorist General Giulio Douhet believed aerial bombing alone would be able to win wars, noting that: "A nation which once loses the command of the air and finds itself subjected to incessant aerial attacks aimed directly at its most vital centers and without the possibility of effective retaliation, this nation, whatever its surface forces may be able to do, must arrive at the conviction that all is useless, that all hope is dead. This conviction spells defeat" (Douhet, p.126). Although his prognostication that aerial bombardment could single-handedly force an enemy to capitulate was not entirely accurate, some of his theories, including the importance of gaining air superiority and bombing strategic sites, still hold water today. American General William "Billy" Mitchell was an acolyte of Douhet's teachings and was one of the most ardent advocates of airpower and a separate air force. He predicted that "future wars… will be conducted by a special class, the air force, as it was by the armored knights in the Middle Ages" (Mitchell, p.19). Like Douhet, not all of Mitchell's prophecies came true, but the advances in aircraft technology and strategy during World War Two helped pave the way for commanders to understand the significance of this new battle space.

These theories, however, were simply just that, and to put them to the test, the "special class" of warfighters and their machines were the ones validating the importance of airpower. Facing the ultimate sacrifice, these airmen overcame many challenges, including enemy fire from the ground and in the air, as well as their own aircraft, which were often rushed into service with minimal testing. The bravery these warriors exhibited in the air cannot be overstated, and their Herculean efforts during World War Two deserve the highest praise.

One way to honor these World War Two heroes is to restore their machines to airworthiness so that they may once again fly in their full glory. Generous benefactors and legions of dedicated volunteers work hard to find, repair, restore, and fly old warbirds. These aircraft serve as a tribute to the sacrifices made by the pilots, aircrew, and maintainers and become an even more poignant reminder of the price of war as fewer World War Two veterans are available to tell their stories. History is often difficult to appreciate if it is only viewed in the context of a textbook but seeing and hearing fully functional aircraft helps people understand the perils involved in the early years of flight, especially during combat. Bringing vintage aircraft back to life helps younger generations appreciate the valiant soldiers who put their lives on the line for their country and hopefully prevents them from making the same mistakes that led to war.

This book will help honor the veterans who flew in World War Two as well as those who are involved in the restoration of their aircraft. The behind-the-scenes work of the mechanics, pilots, and donors is often overlooked by airshow audiences, and they deserve much kudos for preserving history. Civilian owners and operators are the driving force behind warbird rehabilitation, although some government entities, such as the Air Force Heritage Flight Foundation, provide assistance and financial backing. Often certified as charitable organizations, the various groups involved in restoration are constantly on the lookout for volunteers and contributions, so if any aircraft highlighted in this book have provided inspiration, please visit their website and donate!

# CHAPTER 1
# PHOTOGRAPHING RESTORED AIRCRAFT

One of the best times to photograph these glorious aircraft is at airshows. Pilots know that photographers are keen to snap pictures and fly so that their best angles are on display. Of course, the best spot is usually front and center on the runway, which is the target point for most of the maneuvers. Although sometimes pricey, tickets for these spots are always worth it for the experience, and the money spent goes to a good cause. Additionally, many airshows offer premium services including shade, beverages, and exclusive access to performers. To get even closer to the action, some photographers apply for and receive press passes, which allow them to be on the runway during the show. Be sure to request these passes in advance, as spaces do fill up quickly. Airshows will often have pyrotechnic effects during flybys to simulate a bomb run, so be ready to capture the aircraft in flight as well as the "explosions" on the ground. Some of the airshows featured in this book include SkyFair in Everett (Washington), Miramar Airshow in San Diego (California), AIRSHO in Midland (Texas), Wings over Dallas in Dallas (Texas), Planes of Fame in Chino (California), and Wings over Camarillo in Camarillo (California). All these events also provide opportunities to see other types of aircraft in action, including aerobatic biplanes and modern high-performance fighters. No matter the itinerary, it is always an exciting time to go to an airshow!

A major organization involved with warbird restoration is the Commemorative Air Force (CAF), which is a 501(c)(3) charity dedicated to preserve and display historic combat aircraft. While most of its aircraft are World War Two vintage, it also has some postwar aircraft in its inventory, including the T-33 Shooting Star and L-19 Bird Dog. Although headquartered in Dallas, Texas, its chapters, known as wings and squadrons, are spread out over the entirety of the US, from Alaska to Florida. It even has international units, with wings based in the UK, France, and Switzerland. Founded in 1957 by a group of enthusiasts who started out with a single P-51 Mustang, the CAF collection of warbirds has grown to be one of the largest in the world, with over 60 different types and a total of 175 aircraft. With over 13,000 members, the CAF has done well in spreading its message, which is to "recreate, remind and reinforce the lessons learned from the defining moments in American military aviation history." For additional information, visit www.commemorativeairforce.org.

Another great charity that is involved in aircraft restoration is the Collings Foundation, based in Stow, Massachusetts, the goal of which is to "honor the sacrifices made by our veterans that allow us to enjoy our freedom; and to educate the visitors, especially younger Americans, about our national history and heritage." Operating nearly 15 aircraft, the collection includes aircraft from the World War Two era as well as fast jets from the Korean and Vietnam Wars, such as the F-4 Phantom, a rare sight for recent airshows. It is best known for touring the US and showcasing its B-24 Liberator, B-25 Mitchell, and P-51 Mustang during the Wings of Freedom Tour. Although known mostly for its restored aircraft, the Collings Foundation also preserves vintage cars, with over 60 types of automobiles from the first part of the 20th century. The Collings Foundation also runs the American

Heritage Museum, which features a plethora of artifacts, relics, vehicles, and aircraft that played crucial roles in American history from the Revolution to the modern era. To support the Collings Foundation, go to www.collingsfoundation.org.

One of the most exciting places to see restored aircraft is the Flying Heritage and Combat Armor Museum (FHCAM) in Everett, Washington. Created in 2004 by Microsoft cofounder Paul Allen, it boasts 26 restored aircraft and nearly 30 armored vehicles with over 20,000ft$^2$ of display area. Situated at Paine Field airport, the FHCAM offers a unique experience as visitors can watch the aircraft preflight, taxi, and take off from the nearby runways for an up close and personal encounter. The museum hosts a number of events throughout the year, including SkyFair and TankFest, where the FHCAM's aircraft are flown, and vehicles are driven around the premises for the public to watch. Attention to detail is the FHCAM's calling card, including "all aspects of the mechanical systems and all paint schemes and markings," making them one of the most authentic warbird restoration outfits in the world. Unfortunately, the FHCAM has been closed since 2020, but will hopefully reopen soon. Its website is www.flyingheritage.org.

Founded in 1957, the Planes of Fame Air Museum was the first air museum west of the Mississippi and is currently based in Chino. Planes of Fame has over 160 aircraft in its collection, with over 40 that fly on a regular basis. Most of its aircraft are World War Two vintage, but it also has an airworthy F-86 and two MiG-15s, Korean War adversaries. Located at Chino Airport, the museum is open for the public to visit its static displays, and it also publishes a schedule of flights. Annually, the museum puts on an airshow to let "thousands see and hear historic warbirds, vintage aircraft, and aerobatic performers take to the skies." Restoring aircraft is its forte, with current projects including refurbishing a B-17, a Japanese Val dive bomber, and a C-47, with budgets ranging from US$100,000 to US$2,000,000, with the goal of allowing "generations to appreciate our vast aviation heritage." In addition to the aircraft, the museum hosts many restored military vehicles including the M4 Sherman and M5 Stuart tanks. To help the Planes of Fame Air Museum, stop by www.planesoffame.org.

In addition to these outstanding organizations, there are countless numbers of private collectors who allow the public to see their aircraft by bringing them to airshows or loaning them out to museums. Those who restore vintage warbirds are doing so to honor the veterans of history's greatest conflict and to inspire future generations to be passionate about aviation. It is a privilege to see rehabilitated aircraft in flight, to hear the roar of the engines, and to be able to talk to those involved with these aircraft. A debt of gratitude goes out to those who are committed to restoring glory.

*Night Mission* gets ready for a photo pass to salute the crowd.

# CHAPTER 2
# INVADER

Proudly serving across three wars, the Douglas A-26 Invader saw action in World War Two, Korea, and Vietnam as a light bomber and night interdictor. With over 2,500 built, it proved adaptable to many missions, such as ground attack and photo reconnaissance and had an armament of up to eight .50cal M2 Browning machine guns, 10 rockets, and 4,000lb of ordnance in the bomb bay. It has a crew of three, pilot, bombardier, and gunner, a maximum speed of 360mph, and a maximum range of 1,600 miles. Originally flown in 1942, design issues including poor visibility prevented the Invader from seeing combat until 1944, with production of the aircraft ceasing with the end of the war in 1945.

After the outbreak of the Korean War, the Invader was redesignated as the B-26 (not to be confused with the Martin B-26 Marauder) and participated in the first US Air Force (USAF) bombing mission on an airfield near Pyongyang on June 29, 1950 (Horne, p.50). Notably, the Invader was the aircraft used during Captain John Walmsley's heroic Medal of Honor action on September 14, 1951, and his award citation reads as follows:

> While flying a B-26 aircraft on a night combat mission with the objective of developing new tactics, Capt. Walmsley sighted an enemy supply train which had been assigned top priority as a target of opportunity. He immediately attacked, producing a strike which disabled the train, and, when his ammunition was expended, radioed for friendly aircraft in the area to complete destruction of the target. Employing the searchlight mounted on his aircraft, he guided another B-26 aircraft to the target area, meanwhile constantly exposing himself to enemy fire. Directing an incoming B-26 pilot, he twice boldly aligned himself with the target, his searchlight illuminating the area, in a determined effort to give the attacking aircraft full visibility. As the friendly aircraft prepared for the attack, Capt. Walmsley descended into the valley in a low-level run over the target with searchlight blazing, selflessly exposing himself to vicious enemy anti-aircraft fire. In his determination to inflict maximum damage on the enemy, he refused to employ evasive tactics and valiantly pressed forward straight through an intense barrage, thus ensuring complete destruction of the enemy's vitally needed war cargo. While he courageously pressed his attack Capt. Walmsley's plane was hit and crashed into the surrounding mountains, exploding upon impact.

By the end of the Korean War, the Invaders were yet again inactivated.

However, the Invader's tour of duty would not be finished yet, as yet another Asian conflict would call it back to service. As the Vietnam War progressed, a need arose to attack supply lines on the Ho Chi Minh Trail, and the Invader was heavily modified to become the A-26A Counter Invader, serving between 1966 and 1969 in Southeast Asia. The US Central Intelligence Agency (CIA) also used Invaders for training, reconnaissance, close air support, and other clandestine missions, ostensibly to help the South Vietnamese Air Force. The last USAF Invaders were retired in 1972 and were the only American bombers to serve in three wars.

Fortunately, nearly 100 Invaders still survive to this day in varying states of restoration. One such example is the A-26 *Night Mission* flown

An anti-aircraft crew watch as *Night Mission* takes to the sky on another strike against Communist military targets. The light bombers fly day and night missions, attacking enemy transportation and supply targets. The anti-aircraft crews are on round-the-clock watch to protect the base in the event of an enemy air attack. (US Air Force photo)

transport craft. This particular example was even allegedly involved in a drug-running scheme, as Drug Enforcement Agency (DEA) agents had been trying to capture this Invader. Returning it back to the right side of the law, the CAF purchased the Invader in 1977 and initial restoration was completed in 1982. Grounded in 1986 due to mechanical issues, *Night Mission* flew once again in 1988 and has since been active in ground-attack demonstrations at airshows, which include simulated gun and bombing runs. It is always exciting when *Night Mission* flies, because pyrotechnics are sure to follow. The Invader Squadron's website can be found here: https://www.invadersquadron.org/index.php.

*Night Mission* begins its simulated attack run during a CAF-sponsored airshow.

by the Invader Squadron of the CAF, which operates an airworthy Invader and participates in airshows all over the US. Honoring Captain Walmsley, the Invader Squadron has painted its A-26 to the same scheme his aircraft had when he made his fateful flight. Originally built in 1943, with the USAF serial number 41-39427, it was stationed in South Carolina, New Mexico, and California before being stricken in 1950 and sold on the civilian market, eventually becoming an executive

A column of smoke appears as *Night Mission* zooms past its destroyed target, with pyrotechnics providing a sense of realism to the attack.

LEFT: *Night Mission* provides passenger flights with options for cockpit or rear-facing seats available.

BELOW: The eight .50cal M2 Browning machine guns are on full display in the nose, and although they are no longer operational, they still give *Night Mission* a menacing look.

On display during this photo pass are all the guns of *Night Mission*: eight in the nose, three in each wing, and two in the top turret, making this A-26 a very well-armed attack aircraft.

These simulated dogfights show how chaotic air combat can be. Oftentimes, it is difficult to identify who is winning or losing until someone has smoke trailing from their aircraft; a testament to the bravery of the pilots.

# CHAPTER 3
# ZERO

One of the most famous and dreaded fighters, especially at the beginning of World War Two, was the deadly Mitsubishi A6M Zero, which wreaked havoc in the Pacific. Patrolling the skies for the Imperial Japanese Navy, when introduced it was the most feared aircraft combining exceptional maneuverability, range, and firepower, giving even the vaunted Spitfire a run for its money in a dogfight. The low weight and wing loading of the Zero gave it legendary nimbleness and extended range, with Mitsubishi designers using extremely light aluminum alloys in the body, cutting holes in bracing, and sacrificing armor plating. Its early successes prompted the Japanese to build over 10,000 Zeros, the most of any fighter that Japan produced. Using aircraft carriers as floating airfields, Zeros were able to strike nearly everywhere in the Pacific and escorted long-range bombers to targets deep into China and back. The Zero had a 1,100-mile range, which could be extended to 1,600 miles with drop tanks, a full 300 miles further than its early opponent, the Grumman F4F Wildcat. According to famed Zero ace Saburo Sakai, "the Zero was designed to remain in the air on a single flight for a maximum of six or seven hours. We stretched this figure to two to twelve hours and did so on mass formation flights" (Sakai, p.127). This baffled American commanders, who thought the Japanese forces had greater numbers of carriers, as the Zero kept appearing over distant battlefields thought to be inaccessible to fighter escorts. Two 20mm cannons and two 7.7mm machine guns gave the Zero a powerful punch to complement its long legs. Topping out at 330mph, it could keep up with any of its contemporaries before 1943.

Unfortunately, the lighter weight of the Zero came at a heavy price. The lack of armor and self-sealing fuel tanks made them particularly vulnerable to incoming gunfire, particularly later in the war when the US Navy fielded better performing aircraft and updated tactics. Many American pilots noted how easy it was to set fire to a Zero, and the Japanese Navy lost many experienced pilots due to this vulnerability. Naval aviators soon learned to not engage in turning fights with the Zero, but rather to use "boom and zoom" tactics, where they would make diving attacks and use their increased energy to get away from the enemy. With the introduction of the Grumman F6F Hellcat and Vought F4U Corsair, the hunter became the hunted, and the Zero no longer ruled the Pacific skies. Towards the end of the war, Zeros began receiving armor plating and self-sealing fuel tanks, but no additional modifications were made, indicating that the Zero's performance was already at its maximum. In just a few short years, the Zero was dethroned as the best fighter in the Pacific and was eventually relegated to kamikaze attacks.

Because so many Zeros fell victim to American guns, finding intact aircraft has become increasingly difficult. There are only five airworthy Zeros worldwide, and one of the most famous examples is owned by the Southern California Wing of the CAF. Its particular Zero is A6M3 Model 22 *X-133*, produced between 1942 and 1943 to correct issues found in the earlier Model 32. The Model 22 had longer wingtips, folding wings, drop tank capabilities, and a larger internal fuel tank, making it the longest-ranged Zero variant. Its original Sakae engine was the most powerful of all models at 1,130hp, and *X-133* has a replacement Pratt & Whitney R-1830 Twin Wasp engine, which produces about 1,200hp. *X-133* is based on a Zero that was shot down in 1941 and recovered in New Guinea in 1991, and uses additional parts from Zeros found in Russia. Returned to flying status in 1998, *X-133* has been restored to such good condition that it was movie-worthy, flying in the 2001 film *Pearl Harbor* and has wowed audiences who attended its airshows. The cockpit is mostly original, with only minor upgrades made to comply with Federal Aviation Administration (FAA) safety guidelines such as GPS navigation. Director of Maintenance Trace Eubanks notes that a lot of work is required to keep the *X-133* flying, as "The airframe is very light and thin which makes it prone to stress fractures and cracks… Most if not all of the manuals we have on this particular aircraft are written in Japanese. We have two individuals who are in the process of translating much of the documentation. Unfortunately [it] is old school Japanese which makes it difficult to translate." The amount of labor and expertise needed for *X-133* makes it even more imperative to donate to the CAF so that history stays alive. Although flying for the Axis powers, seeing *X-133* in action drives home the point that soldiers on both sides must have had incredible courage to fly these aircraft into combat. More information on *X-133* can be found at https://www.cafsocal.com/our-aircrafts/our-aircraft-and-history/mitsubishi-a6m3-zero/.

The CAF's Zero, *X-133*, sits on the ramp before its airshow mission.

*X-133* begins taxiing to the runway before taking off. The pilot, Rob Hertberg, is seen checking his instruments for safety.

**ABOVE LEFT:** *X-133* plays an important part in showing what it was like to be under enemy attack and the courage needed to defend against such a high-performance aircraft.

**ABOVE RIGHT:** As a part of the airshow, *X-133* simulates dogfighting American aircraft, and when "hit," smoke is deployed to simulate aircraft damage.

**LEFT:** After another successful mission chasing around other restored warbirds, the *X-133* comes in for a landing.

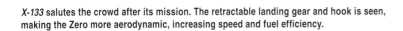

*X-133* salutes the crowd after its mission. The retractable landing gear and hook is seen, making the Zero more aerodynamic, increasing speed and fuel efficiency.

The belly of *X-133* is on full display as it banks away from the audience.

The CAF's Texan, *Ace in the Hole,* makes a pass over the show center, putting its magnificent color scheme on display.

# CHAPTER 4
# TEXAN

Known affectionately as "The Pilotmaker," the North American AT-6 Texan was an advanced trainer for the US and British Commonwealth during World War Two and has trained more pilots than any other aircraft in the history of flight. Legendary pilots including Chuck Yeager and Bud Anderson, who each achieved ace status by downing 11.5 and 16.25 aircraft, respectively, sharpened their skills in the Texan. The Royal Air Force (RAF) and its Commonwealth cousins also flew the Texan, known as the Harvard overseas, to familiarize pilots with American aircraft that had different controls than British ones. There are two seats in the Texan cockpit, with the instructor sitting in the rear while the student sits up front for a better view. Built by North American Aviation, the Texan was first flown in 1935, and over 15,000 were built until production stopped in 1952. With a 600hp Pratt & Whitney R-1340 engine, the Texan's top speed was a lethargic 208mph, and although not fleet-footed by any stretch of the imagination, it was nimble enough to give the student a feel for most basic dogfighting maneuvers and was able to carry guns and bombs to practice strafing and bombing attacks.

One of the main reasons for the Texan's success was its versatility and ease of use. No fewer than 50 variants of the Texan were produced for use with the US Army Air Force (USAAF), US Navy, RAF, Royal Canadian Air Force (RCAF), Belgian Air Force, and many other air forces around the world. Costing approximately US$450 at the time of production (approximately US$10,000 in 2022), the Texan made economic sense to mass produce and operate. It was also easy to maintain and repair, making it a popular choice for aircraft restoration, with at least 500 in the hands of private owners. Although long since retired, the Texan's legacy as a trainer lives on in the Beechcraft T-6 Texan II, the current trainer of choice for the USAF, US Navy, RCAF and Hellenic Air Force. Nearly 100 years later, pilots for fifth generation aircraft are still learning the ropes on a Texan!

There are many excellent restored airworthy Texans today, and some even fly painted as Japanese aircraft to simulate Zeros. The examples shown in this book are from the Houston Wing of the CAF, showing its AT-6A *Ace in the Hole*, and Mr. Malcom B. Liang flying its silver AT-6G. Fittingly, these Texans participate primarily in airshows located in Texas and are a staple in the Wings over Dallas show. For a donation, *Ace in the Hole* can take passengers up for a joyride. The Houston Wing provides amateur aviation enthusiasts the chance to get up close and personal with a bona fide warbird without having to spend the astronomical costs of finding, restoring, maintaining, training, and flying the Texan. At approximately US$150,000 to purchase, buying a Texan is out of reach for most people, but through the CAF, the Houston Wing can make that dream a reality for more people while also supporting veterans and remembering the history. Because Texans are relatively common, large formations are possible and are an awe-inspiring sight to see, with some gatherings of over 20 aircraft. The T-6 community is large and has evolved over the years from pilots buying a relatively cheap surplus military aircraft to dedicated collectors trying to restore the aircraft with as much authenticity as possible. While not the fastest or sleekest aircraft on the airshow circuit, the Texan is without a doubt one of the most important aircraft in early aviation history, as it trained legends, aces, and pioneers. The *Ace in the Hole*'s website is https://www.houstonwing.org/at-6-texan/.

John Collver's Texan, *War Dog*, makes a loop with smoke trailing for dramatic effect.

This T-6G Texan pounds the air with its propellers pushing it across the sky at a blistering 140mph.

*Texas Raiders* has distinctive, red-tipped wings and tail, identifying it as part of the 533rd Bombardment Squadron.

# CHAPTER 5

# FLYING FORTRESS

Bristling with 13 .50cal M2 Browning machine guns and carrying a payload of up to 8,000lb, the Boeing B-17 lived up to its name of the "Flying Fortress." It was one of the war's most iconic aircraft, representing American military and industrial strength and symbolizing the resolve of the Allied airmen. With four Wright R-1870-97 1,200hp engines, the Flying Fortress had a combat range of almost 2,000 miles, meaning it was able to strike all the way to Berlin from bases in England. There were ten aviators on board, including the pilot, copilot, navigator, flight engineer/top gunner, radio operator, bombardier/ nose gunner, two waist gunners, ball turret gunner, and tail gunner. The ultimate B-17 model was the B-17G, which was able to fly at a speed of 290mph at over 35,000ft, putting it out of range of some Axis fighters, such as early models of the Japanese Zero. Flying Fortresses were deployed in both the Pacific

**Medal of Honor recipient Lieutenant Joseph Sarnoski. (Photo courtesy of US Air Force)**

and European theaters, but, by 1943, all B-17s were slated to fly in Europe. The B-17 dropped more bombs on Axis powers than any other airframe, including over 40 percent of the total tonnage on Germany, and took heavy casualties, with over 45,000 American servicemembers being killed or wounded on the B-17. Although a steep price to pay, the Flying Fortresses were able to bring an end to the war more quickly by destroying key strategic installations and resources, such as manufacturing and oil storage facilities. Additionally, with the introduction of the P-51 Mustang to provide a long-range escort, it seemed like nothing could stop the B-17 from bringing the end to Nazi Germany.

Crew members described the Flying Fortress as a tough and reliable aircraft, able to take substantial damage and still return home. A testament to the B-17s ruggedness was the *All American*, a B-17F, which suffered a mid-air collision with a Bf 109 and nearly lost its entire tail but was able to land safely in friendly territory without any injuries to its crew. Another famous B-17 mission was when *Old 666* fended off over 20 Japanese Zeros during a reconnaissance mission for over 40 minutes and was able to complete its photographing run. For their efforts, two of the crew members, Second Lieutenant Joseph Sarnoski and Captain Jay Zeamer were awarded the Medal of Honor, with Sarnoski making the ultimate sacrifice for his crew. Lieutenant Sarnoski's posthumous citation reads:

When a coordinated frontal attack by the enemy extensively damaged his bomber, and seriously injured 5 of the crew, 2d Lt. Sarnoski, though wounded, continued firing and shot down 2 enemy planes. A 20-millimeter shell which burst in the nose of the bomber knocked him into the catwalk under the cockpit. With indomitable fighting spirit, he crawled back to his post and kept on firing until he collapsed on his guns.

In total, 17 B-17 crew members received the Medal of Honor, showing that the Flying Fortress was frequently in harm's way and its pilots, gunners, navigators, and bombardiers were up to the task of defending freedom.

B-17 *Texas Raiders* rolled off the factory line in California at the very end of World War Two and was never sent into action. Although slated for scrap, in July 1945, the US Navy selected it to test out its early Airborne Early Warning and Control System (AWACS) during Project *Cadillac II* until 1955, making it a pioneer and predecessor to the modern Northrop Grumman E-2 Hawkeye carrier-borne AWACS. Redesignated as a PB-1, *Texas Raiders* was fitted with an AN/APS-20 radar system, an advanced design for its time that could detect moving aerial targets and give some command-and-control ability. After its tour of duty across the US with the Navy, a private company saved it from the scrap heap and *Texas Raiders* provided aerial photography until 1967, when the Gulf Coast Wing of the CAF bought it and turned it into a flying museum, where it remains the oldest flying B-17 museum in the world. *Texas Raiders* has provided flights to thousands of passengers since 2001 and has educated millions who attend airshows and events. Out of nearly 13,000 built, today only five B-17s fly on a regular basis, making *Texas Raiders* a unique sight. *Texas Raiders'* webpage is https://b17texasraiders.org/index.php/about-b-17-texas-raiders.

**ABOVE:** The paintings of the bombs on the nose of *Texas Raiders* indicate the number of missions it has flown, and at this snapshot in time, it had completed 28 sorties.

**LEFT:** The ball turret underneath *Texas Raiders* is shown here; a claustrophobic and dangerous position on the aircraft.

*Texas Raiders* banks left to give the audience a good view of the top side of the aircraft.

Smoke belches from *Texas Raiders*, which has one wheel down as it simulates damage from an air attack.

This type of display shows how deadly being a bomber crew could be, with the aircraft on fire and only one wheel able to come down, the options for a safe landing are limited.

Fortunately, the B-17 was a tough airplane and could take some serious damage to get its crews home safely.

Don Boccaccio expertly pilots the B-24 into the air to begin its airshow display.

# CHAPTER 6
# LIBERATOR

Aptly named for its role in World War Two, the Consolidated B-24 Liberator was the most produced heavy bomber and American military aircraft in history, with over 18,000 aircraft, and it saw action with all branches in both the Pacific and European theaters. Its long range enabled it to provide extended protection for convoys during the Battle of the Atlantic and strike strategic targets deep in the heart of Germany and Japan. The low drag and shoulder-mounted wings were key contributors to its 3,000-mile range and 8,000lb maximum bomb load. Four Pratt & Whitney R-1830 engines produced 1,200hp each, giving the Liberator a top speed of nearly 300mph. Liberators typically had a crew of 11: a pilot, copilot, navigator, radio operator, bombardier, and six gunners. The first prototype flew in 1939, and B-24s were accepted into the USAAF by 1941, immediately deploying all over the world from Burma to Egypt to England. Like the Japanese Zero, the Liberator traded durability for range and speed, and was particularly susceptible to fires started by

**Medal of Honor recipient Lieutenant Lloyd Hughes. (Photo courtesy of US Air Force)**

bullets and flak. Inside, the gunners had to sit on the floor when not engaged and heaters used on board were not reliable, making for a cold and bumpy ride. During the initial production, manufacturing processes were not followed correctly, causing drafts in the air and fuel leaks on the ground. As a result, although a capable bomber, Liberators were not as popular as Flying Fortresses among American airmen.

Despite its drawbacks, the Liberator was able to make its mark during the war, taking part in some of the most dangerous missions of the conflict. The most infamous of these raids took place on August 1, 1943, over Ploesti, Romania, when there was an attempt to knock out oil refineries fueling the German war machine. Of 177 Liberators dispatched, 54 did not return, and their objectives were not completed as the attack failed to significantly diminish the capacity of the refineries. Over 600 airmen were lost, and the date became known as "Bloody Sunday," and "though the Liberators had been led by experienced group commanders, they had difficulty finding their way, many formations missed their mark, and the losses were much too high" (Mets, p.271). Five Medals of Honor were awarded; the highest number of any air mission during the war. One such recipient was Second Lieutenant Lloyd Hughes, whose Liberator, which had been damaged during a previous bomb run, was leaking fuel into flames below. Instead of turning back, Hughes chose to do the following:

2d Lt. Hughes, motivated only by his high conception of duty which called for the destruction of his assigned target at any cost, did not elect to make a forced landing or turn back from the attack. Instead, rather than jeopardize the formation and the success of the attack, he unhesitatingly entered the blazing area and dropped his bomb load with great precision. After successfully bombing the objective, his aircraft emerged from the conflagration with the left wing aflame. Only then did he attempt a forced landing, but because of the advanced stage of the fire enveloping his aircraft the plane crashed and was consumed.

The brave men who flew during Bloody Sunday were avenged in 1944, when further air raids and ground campaigns completely cut off the flow of oil to the Third Reich.

Flying for the CAF Airpower Squadron, based in Dallas, Texas, B-24 *Diamond Lil* has had a long history. Rolling out of the factory in 1940, *Diamond Lil* was originally slated to serve in the French Air Force but was diverted to the RAF after the fall of France to Nazi occupation. The RAF used the airframe as a trainer; however, it was damaged during a landing and sent to San Diego for extensive repairs in 1940. *Diamond Lil* was returned to service in 1942 as a transport, hauling vital supplies between factories, and it was also used as a test bed for improvements to the flight controls. After the war, *Diamond Lil* was converted to a transport for various private companies and was acquired by the CAF in 1968 and was painted in its current colors honoring the 98th Bomb Group, which participated in the Ploesti Raid. Despite various mechanical issues stemming from age, the members of the CAF did an excellent job of fundraising to keep *Diamond Lil* flying throughout the country. More information about *Diamond Lil* can be found at https://www.airpowersquadron.org/b-24-liberator.

***Diamond Lil* soars overhead, proudly flaunting that it is part of the US Army Air Force (USAAF). Its color scheme accurately portrays early USAAF livery.**

RIGHT: The folding landing gear helped streamline the aircraft, as its wheels were flush with the underside of the wing, increasing fuel efficiency and range.

BELOW: Offering rides to the public, *Diamond Lil* gives audiences across the country a unique way to experience history.

This fantastic top view of *Number 810* highlights the top turret with its two .50cal machine guns.

# CHAPTER 7
# MITCHELL

William "Billy" Mitchell was one of the preeminent pioneers in American air power and received the posthumous honor of having the North American B-25 named after him, an aircraft that participated in one of the most famous air missions in history and changed the course of World War Two. Introduced in 1941, the Mitchell was originally designed as a medium bomber; however, it evolved into a gunship, reconnaissance aircraft, and even an anti-submarine aircraft fitted with search radars. The B-25 was exported to the United Kingdom, Canada, Australia, the Netherlands, the Soviet Union, and China to fight against the Axis and predominantly fought in the Pacific theater. A crew of five operated the Mitchell: pilot, navigator/bombardier, flight engineer/gunner, radio operator/gunner, and tail gunner. Two Wright R-2600 engines gave the Mitchell 1,700hp each and a top speed of 270mph. As a bomber, the Mitchell could carry up to 3,000lb of bombs, and as a gunship, it could be outfitted with 18 .50cal machine guns, eight rockets, and even a 75mm cannon! Due to the reduced visibility of the jungle canopies over many Pacific battlefields, low-level attacks were more effective and accurate than traditional bombing, and the B-25 was a perfect candidate for these types of assaults. Flying at treetop level exposed the B-25 to enemy anti-aircraft fire, but, fortunately, the Mitchell was designed to take significant punishment, and crew members appreciated its durability.

In an amazing display of courage and airmanship, the B-25B Mitchell was the aircraft flown during the "Doolittle Raid" in 1942. Looking for a way to strike back at the Japanese after Pearl Harbor, Colonel James Doolittle led 16 B-25s to attack targets on the Japanese mainland, including Tokyo, after taking off from the aircraft carrier USS *Hornet*. Doolittle selected the B-25 over the B-18 Bolo, B-23 Dragon, and B-26 Marauder because it had the right combination of range, wingspan, and capacity. The B-25 was not designed to take off from an aircraft carrier, but with the help of a determined crew and the flexibility of the Mitchell, all 16 bombers were able to complete the mission. After taking off from the Hornet, Doolittle's men dropped their ordnance on factories and military targets and continued to China and ditched there (one aircraft flew to the Soviet Union instead), being rescued later. Although not significant in terms of damage caused, the Doolittle Raid provided a massive psychological boost to the American public and caused the Japanese to push forward an attack at Midway as retribution; a battle which changed the course of history. For his efforts in the attack, Doolittle was promoted to Brigadier General and received the Medal of Honor, the citation of which read "With the apparent certainty of being forced to land in enemy territory or to perish at sea, Gen. Doolittle personally led a squadron of Army bombers, manned by volunteer crews, in a highly destructive raid on the Japanese mainland."

Fortunately for aircraft enthusiasts, there are many B-25s that are still airworthy. The FHCAM has beautifully restored a B-25J named *Number 810*, representing an aircraft from the 490th Bomb Squadron that was shot down on its 116th mission to attack Japanese supply lines in the Pacific. The original B-25J started life in Kansas City in 1944 and served as a trainer until the end of the war, where it was delivered to the RCAF. In 1961, it was sold

The original VMB-612 #3 aircraft is seen here. Of note is the radar in the nose used to find enemy ships at night with the PBJ (Patrol Bomber-J) firing unguided rockets to interdict supply lines. (Photo courtesy of Earnest Henderson and the Devil Dog Squadron).

*Devil Dog* is configured and painted to represent a plane that was lost in the Pacific during WWII - #3 of the VMB-612 Squadron. It went out on its 23rd mission and never returned. Our plane was built in late 1944 and was used for training on the west coast. At the end of the war, all armament was removed, and it was sold to a private company in Rockdale, TX – the Rockdale Flying Service. They had four flying B-25s and one that was used for spare parts. Those planes were used to carry cargo to Central and South American mining operations. The business wound down and the planes sat at the Rockdale airport in deteriorating condition. The CAF acquired one of those planes in the late 60's, flew it to Harlingen (the CAF HQ at that time) and began the restoration. One of the people involved with the restoration was part of VMB-612 so they made the decision to configure it as a PBJ with that squadron's livery and the #3. Of note, most of the planes in the VMB-612 squadron did not have the complement of 50-caliber guns in the nose and side blisters like our plane. Instead, they were part of a then top-secret project with radar mounted in the nose that could find ships at sea then launch non-guided rockets at them. Most of those missions were flown at night. According to our records, the #3 plane sank 3 supply ships and one warship (type unknown).

to a Canadian oil company and converted to a water-carrying firefighting aircraft. In 1999, the FHCAM bought it and restored it as *Number 810*, flying it over the Pacific northwest.

Another noteworthy B-25, named *Devil Dog*, is owned and operated by the Devil Dog Squadron of the CAF. The US Marine Corps also used B-25s and designated them as the PBJs (Patrol Bomber-J) for night attacks against enemy supply lines. As Crew Chief Earnie Henderson explains:

Lieutenant Colonel Jack Cram, Commander of VMB-12, continues: "[T]he Navy fly boys used their Patrol Bombers to keep the Japanese shipping 'honest' during the day. We used our rockets and radar to zap them if they attempted to run supplies at night. The success of our mission is a matter of record, with many thousands of tons of Japanese shipping damaged or destroyed" (Honeycutt, p.372). *Devil Dog* remains one of the most active restored warbirds in the world. Additional information on *Devil Dog* is available at https://devildogsquadron.com/pages/home.

The CAF's *Devil Dog* flashes by the audience and shows off its fantastic blue paint job.

Bristling with guns from nose to tail and with ordnance in the bomb-bay, *Devil Dog* packs a huge wallop and was used to attack enemy ground targets and shipping.

**ABOVE LEFT:** *Devil Dog* provides rides for passengers, and one can be seen through the starboard waist-gun port.

**ABOVE RIGHT:** *Number 810* of the FHCAM is seen flying overhead with its bomb-bay doors open, giving the audience a view of its deadly capabilities.

**LEFT:** The "3" on the side indicates that it was the third aircraft in the flight. Unfortunately, the aircraft it represents was shot down in the Pacific.

**ABOVE LEFT:** All aspects of the B-25 are covered, including the tail, as seen with these two M2 Browning machine guns, which will defend against a trailing adversary.

**ABOVE RIGHT:** *Number 810* zooms away from the audience and prepares for another pass.

**RIGHT:** *Number 810* has a glass nose, differentiating it from *Devil Dog*, which enabled more accurate strikes from the bombardier.

The CAF's *"FIFI"* soars overhead, showing its two ventral turrets that could be controlled by a single fire control officer.

# CHAPTER 8
# SUPERFORTRESS

The Boeing B-29 Superfortress brought about the end to World War Two and the beginning of the nuclear age. Though it is best known for being the only airframe to drop nuclear weapons in anger, the Superfortress was also an incredible high-altitude strategic bomber as well as a low-level fire bomber and naval minelayer. With some of the latest technology on board, the B-29 boasted a pressurized cabin and a computer-controlled fire-control system, which enabled the gunner to remotely operate four turrets at a time. The pressurization allowed the crew to move without carrying oxygen bottles and heaters to work more efficiently, since the extreme cold temperatures required B-17 crew members to wear electrically heated suits that "had wires, much like the electric blanket on a bed... should any of the wires burn out, a crew member was in line for serious frost bite" (Unruh, p.31). The computer-controlled guns provided accurate and deadly defensive fire, both of which were very much appreciated by the airmen. Development cost over US$3bn, making it an even more expensive weapons system than the atomic bomb. Boeing built nearly 4,000 aircraft in a two-year span between 1942 and 1944. It had a massive range of over 3,000 miles, perfect for the island-hopping campaign in the Pacific, while also being able to fly at a maximum speed of 360mph and carrying up to 20,000lb of bombs. Like the Flying Fortress, the B-29 bristled with guns, including ten .50cal machine guns. Four Wright R-3350-23 supercharged engines provided 2,200hp each, spinning the four adjustable propellers at 2,600rpm.

Superfortresses devastated Japanese cities through intense firebombing campaigns – one raid could kill more people than an atomic bomb, destroying Imperial Japan's ability to produce war materiel. Additionally, the B-29 proved very adept at mining Japanese harbors and shipping routes, further blocking their ability to keep the war effort going. Most famously, B-29s *Enola Gay* and *Bockscar* dropped nuclear weapons on Hiroshima and Nagasaki, respectively, forcing Japan to surrender after just a few days of deliberation. Another notable B-29 mission occurred on April 12, 1945, when Staff Sergeant Henry Erwin threw an errant phosphorous bomb out of his aircraft to save his crew, suffering excruciating burns. His Medal of Honor citation reads:

Among the phosphoresce bombs launched by S/Sgt. Erwin, 1 proved faulty, exploding in the launching chute, and shot back into the interior of the aircraft, striking him in the face. The burning phosphoresce obliterated his nose and completely blinded him. Smoke filled the plane, obscuring the vision of the pilot. S/Sgt. Erwin realized that the aircraft and crew would be lost if the burning bomb remained in the plane. Without regard for his own safety, he picked it up and feeling his way, instinctively, crawled around the gun turret and headed for the copilot's window. He found the navigator's table obstructing his passage. Grasping the burning bomb between his forearm and body, he unleashed the spring lock and raised the table. Struggling through the narrow passage he stumbled forward into the smoke-filled pilot's compartment. Groping with his burning hands, he located the window and threw the bomb out. Completely aflame, he fell back upon the floor. The smoke cleared, the pilot, at 300 feet, pulled the plane out of its dive. S/Sgt. Erwin's gallantry and heroism above and beyond the call of duty saved the lives of his comrades.

After the war, B-29s continued their strategic bombing mission in Korea, and although vulnerable to the new Soviet MiG-15, Superfortresses excelled at night interdiction strikes. The USAF retired the last B-29 variant in 1965 but continued to fly as the Tupolev Tu-4 Bull, an unlicensed and reverse-engineered Soviet copy, which flew for the Chinese People's Liberation Army Air Force until 1988. Long since retired, the B-29s legacy still lives on through the B-52 Stratofortress, one of the longest serving aircraft in the world and a symbol of American nuclear strength.

There are 26 surviving copies of the B-29 today, only two of which are airworthy. One static display is at the Travis AFB Air Museum, and more information can be found in Key Publishing's book, *Travis Air Force Base*. The CAF's Airpower Squadron operates one of the two flying B-29s,

known as *"FIFI"*, which has been a staple on the airshow circuit since 1974. *"FIFI"* began life in Washington and served as an administrative aircraft until 1958, when it was repurposed as a target on the bombing range at China Lake Naval Air Weapons Station in California. In 1971, a CAF pilot flying for the National Guard spotted it from the air, and the CAF negotiated its release from the USAF and US Navy. After three years of restoration efforts, *"FIFI"* was finally airworthy and began its tour around the country at airshows. In 2006, the engines needed to be replaced, and four years and US$3m later, *"FIFI"* flew again, a much safer and more efficient aircraft. Providing flights to passengers helps fund the maintenance and keeps the history of this magnificent aircraft alive. To book a seat on *"FIFI"*, visit https://www.cafb29b24. org/b-29-superfortress.

ABOVE: As *"FIFI"* zooms away on takeoff, the rear gun turret is seen. This was operated by a gunner, who could visually track their target, rather than a remote operator.

RIGHT: Because the B-29s were pressurized, the entire fuselage was sealed so that the crew members could move around more comfortably. This resulted in a change from the B-17, in which there were no open waist gunner windows.

OPPOSITE: A unique feature of *"FIFI"* is that each of its engines is emblazoned with the first name of a Hollywood actress of the era: "Rita" (Hayworth), "Betty" (Grable), "Mitzi" (Gaynor), and "Ingrid" (Bergman).

OPPOSITE: It is absolutely breathtaking to see *"FIFI"* fly overhead and to also see the size of the shadow it casts.

RIGHT: The dedicated volunteers that help maintain *"FIFI"* do an excellent job of keeping it clean, even keeping the exhaust ports shiny.

# CHAPTER 9

# VALIANT

Although not as well-known as the T-6 Texan, the Vultee BT-13 Valiant played a critical role in the training and development of rookie Allied pilots. Each American military branch used the Valiant to teach young aviators more advanced flying techniques, as it was more powerful and maneuverable than basic trainers and could challenge the student with its less forgiving controls. Like most trainers, it had a crew of two, with the instructor pilot in the back having identical controls as the student in the front. The BT-13 was originally outfitted with a Pratt & Whitney R-985 450hp engine, and those that used the Wright R-975 engine were redesignated as the BT-15. It was pejoratively known as the "Vibrator," because it tended to noticeably shake during all stages of flight, and sometimes the vibrations would be difficult to control near stall speeds. The Valiant had a top speed of 180mph and a 700-mile range. Over 9,500 Valiants were built between 1939 and 1945, after which most were sold for pennies on the dollar and any leftovers were scrapped.

Because Valiants were relatively cheap to buy after World War Two, they became a common collector's item among aviation enthusiasts, with over 50 survivors around the world and at least 16 airworthy examples. Valiants are often repainted to represent the Japanese Aichi D3A Val dive-bomber during airshows and movies, most recently seen in the 2001 romantic war drama *Pearl Harbor*. One of the CAF's signature airshow displays is the *Tora! Tora! Tora!* reenactment, which shows how the US became involved in World War Two. As authentic Japanese aircraft are difficult to come by, the Valiant stands in as a substitute to add to the realism of the flight. Valiant *41-21178* is a movie star, having been used by MGM in the 1970 war movie *Tora! Tora! Tora!* and later being restored by the CAF to an original BT-13 Valiant.

**OPPOSITE: Thanks to the rear seat of the CAF's Valiant, passenger flights are available and provide a unique photo opportunity.**

# CHAPTER 10

# EXPEDITOR

One of the most versatile Allied aircraft in World War Two was the Beechcraft C-45 Expeditor, known in the civilian world as the Model 18. Produced by Beechcraft for over 30 years, 9,000 examples were built for missions ranging from executive transport, utility, cargo, training, reconnaissance and even light bombing, with variants that used floats and skis to land on water and snow, respectively. For the USAAF, almost all bombardiers and navigators trained with the Expeditor before moving on to heavier aircraft, making it a vital aircraft. The C-45 had two Pratt & Whitney R-985 engines, one on each wing, which produced 450hp each, giving the Expeditor a top speed of 225mph and a 1,200-mile range. It also had a unique twin-tail configuration, which enabled better rudder control at slow speeds. The USAAF, US Navy, RAF, and RCAF all used C-45s in a transport role, while the Republic of China used them as bombers, designated as M18Rs, with at least one of them being flown by the famous "Flying Tigers." It was outfitted with two .30cal turret-mounted machine guns and could deliver a payload of up to 1,000lb.

There are over 200 flying Model 18s in the US alone, due in part to its relatively low cost and ease of handling. One such example is *210904* of the CAF's Cimarron Strip Wing, which is located in Guymon, Oklahoma. It was originally built in 1943 as a C-45B and rebuilt in 1954 as a C-45H, after which it was loaned to the US Navy. This Expeditor was then given to the University of Texas for research purposes and then bought by the CAF in 1991 and has since been operated by the Cimarron Strip Wing and spends much of its time in Texas. Although a support aircraft, the Expeditor was an important aircraft to keep the war effort going, and its legacy as an adaptable aircraft lives on through its civilian operators, who continue to find new uses for the C-45.

OPPOSITE: This Expeditor delivers the message that it takes more than just fighters and bombers to win a war: it takes logistics and cargo aircraft too!

Invasion stripes helped identify Allied aircraft to prevent friendly fire. Like most other C-47s, *That's All, Brother* had its stripes hastily painted on, and, as such, the lines are not perfectly straight, a detail that the CAF did not overlook.

# CHAPTER 11
# SKYTRAIN

Arguably one of the most important transport aircraft in history, the Douglas C-47 Skytrain provided valuable cargo supplies and paratroop drops in all theaters of World War Two while continuing to serve in a deadly role as a gunship in Vietnam. The C-47 draws its lineage from the Douglas Aircraft Company's DC-3, which was originally built as a passenger airline. Compared to its contemporaries, the DC-3 had better range, speed, and comfort for its passengers, and it was able to make cross country trips faster and with fewer stops. The DC-3 helped make air travel more glamorous and fashionable with comfortable seating or bunks, all while looking sleek and stylish in its metallic silver livery. By 1938, "it was estimated that 80 percent of all U.S. passengers traveled in DC–3s" (Bilstein, p.15). In 1941, the USAAF accepted a modified version of the DC-3 as its primary transport aircraft and designated it as the C-47 Skytrain. Like the B-24 Liberator, the Skytrain used Pratt & Whitney R-1830 engines that provided 1,200hp each, giving the C-47 a top speed of 220mph and a range of 1,600 miles while carrying 6,000lb of cargo or 28 fully loaded paratroopers. Supreme Allied Commander General Dwight Eisenhower noted that the C-47 was one of the keys to victory, stating that, "Four things won the Second World War – the bazooka, the Jeep, the atom bomb, and the C-47" (Bilstein, p.17).

Operation *Overlord*, the Allied invasion of France at Normandy, was the most famous of all the C-47 missions and, along with towed gliders, these aircraft dropped over 13,000 paratroopers behind enemy lines on D-Day. Although often scattered miles away from their designated drop zones, these brave soldiers did their part to cut German communications lines, secure logistics routes, and generally sow discord and confusion in the enemy's rear echelon. Skytrains also helped airlift over 35,000 troops and their support equipment during the infamous Operation *Market Garden*, which ultimately failed due to the paratroopers being unsupported. Although not a strategic success, the C-47s proved their worth during this mission by ferrying an unprecedented number of men and materiel to a combat zone. The Skytrain also served in a humanitarian role, providing vital supplies to those trapped in West Berlin during Operation *Vittles*, better known as the "Berlin Airlift." Although many had been sold off after World War Two, the USAF maintained a sizeable fleet of C-47s, converting at least 50 of them to the AC-47 Spooky variant, in which a Skytrain was outfitted with three M134 miniguns, which fired from the left side of the aircraft to provide close air support to ground units. One AC-47 mission resulted in the award of the Medal of Honor to Airman First Class John Levitow, who threw an activated aerial flare out of his damaged AC-47 despite over 40 shrapnel wounds and a concussion, saving his aircraft and crew members.

Lieutenant Colonel John M. Donalson spearheaded the charge for Operation *Overlord* by flying the lead C-47 on June 5, 1944, over Normandy. His aircraft was known as *That's All, Brother* and paved the way for the next 800 Skytrains to make their way to France. After participating in all the other major airborne campaigns of the war, including Operation *Market Garden*, *That's All, Brother* was sold on the civilian market and changed hands numerous times before ending up in a Wisconsin boneyard, where it was slated to be converted to a

BT-67, a modernized version of the DC-3. Fortunately, its serial number, 42-92847, was found, and its significance discovered. The CAF took possession of the aircraft and contracted Basler Turbo Conversions to restore the aircraft to its original condition. Normally, Basler converts old DC-3s to retain about 30 percent of the original parts, but, in this case, it was able to restore 85 percent of *That's All, Brother*, with the rest being sourced from other World War Two vintage parts, making the aircraft nearly original, including the paint shades. After over 20,000 man-hours and US$330,000 spent, *That's All, Brother* flew again in 2017 in Texas and was brought over the Atlantic to participate in the 75th anniversary of the D-Day landings in 2019, once again leading the charge over the English Channel in a reenactment. A feature-length documentary was filmed about the restoration process and can be found here: https://www.planeresurrection.co.uk/thats-all-brother.

Like many other CAF aircraft, *That's All, Brother* offers passenger rides, allowing the public to relive the historic D-Day flight.

Banking in across the sky, *That's All, Brother* gives the audience a glimpse of what it might have looked like on D-Day.

This would have been the view of the other C-47s on D-Day, as *That's All, Brother* was the lead aircraft of the assault.

*That's All, Brother* flies over the beaches of Normandy, France, on June 8, 2019. Originally, *That's All, Brother* dropped 101st Airborne troops during the invasion of Normandy, on June 6, 1944. (US Air Force photo by Senior Airman Devin M. Rumbaugh)

The Flying Heritage and Combat Armor Museum's (FHCAM) Mosquito has nose markings indicating that it has shot down three German and two Japanese aircraft.

# CHAPTER 12
# MOSQUITO

Originally designed as a simple, fast, light bomber, the de Havilland DH.98 Mosquito developed into a Swiss Army knife for the RAF, with missions ranging from night fighter to photo reconnaissance to freeing prisoners of war from German captors. The Mosquito was made mostly out of wood, including its frame, giving it the nickname the "Wooden Wonder," which reduced weight and increased speed and payload. Fabric was also incorporated in many areas, further lightening the aircraft. Able to fly at over 400mph, the Mosquito was one of the fastest aircraft in the world. Two Rolls-Royce Merlin engines gave the Mosquito its legendary speed, propelling it with over 1,700hp each. Although the combination of armament was limitless depending on the mission, a fighter-bomber version of the Mosquito could carry four .303cal machine guns, four 20mm cannons, and 1,000lb of bombs in the bomb bay, packing a powerful punch against targets both in the air and on the ground. The Mosquito also had a long range of 1,300 miles, making it a great candidate for deep interdiction missions. Over 7,500 Mosquitos were built between 1940 and 1950, due in part to the ease of wooden and fabric construction.

The Mosquito has become an extremely popular aircraft in the public eye because of some of the dangerous and exhilarating missions its crews performed during World War Two, spawning movie blockbusters such as *633 Squadron*. One such daring mission was Operation *Jericho*, in which Mosquitos attempted to free prisoners at Amiens Prison in German-occupied France. Mosquitos flew extremely low and attempted to bomb the prison in precise locations in order to blow holes in walls and open cells with shockwaves, while French Resistance members would

standby and collect the freed prisoners. Unfortunately, the raid had mixed results, as many prisoners were killed in the initial bombings, and many who did escape were recaptured. Nevertheless, the bravery of the Mosquito crews was put on display, over 100 prisoners were freed, and the intelligence they provided was invaluable in outing members of the Gestapo. Another shining example of bravery in a Mosquito was performed by Wing Commander Leonard Cheshire, who received the Victoria Cross in recognition for his many Mosquito missions, including one where he marked targets at a Munich railyard for the following Lancaster bombers to destroy. This dangerous mission pushed the Mosquito and crew to its limits, but, through his brilliant leadership, the raid was successful, and all four of his Mosquitos were able to make it back to base. Night intercepts were also a big part of the Mosquito's missions, and its performance stood out enough for Marshal of the Royal Air Force Sholto Douglas to comment "along with the greatly improved techniques which were by then being employed by the night fighter crews, [the Mosquito] was quite enough to cope with any of the enemy bombers" (Douglas, p.510–11).

The FHCAM has one of the best examples of an airworthy Mosquito, flying a T.Mk.III, serial TV959. It was constructed in 1945 as a trainer and served with the RAF until 1963, during which time it was used in the film *633 Squadron* for ground and cockpit scenes. It was then transferred to the world-famous Imperial War Museum London until 1988, after which it was sold to The Fighter Collection, a European aircraft restoration collective. TV959 was then traded to the FHCAM and sent to New Zealand for restoration, where it was returned to airworthiness in 2016 and has been flying ever since. Although originally a trainer, TV959 was modified to look like the FB.Mk.VI fighter-bomber version of the Mosquito, including in paint job and exterior additions. The goal of many of these restoration projects is to educate people about the importance of history, and TV959 has done that throughout its entire career, piquing interest in World War Two through movies and airshows alike. More information about TV959 can be found at the FHCAM's website: http://flyingheritage.org/Explore/The-Collection/Britain/de-Havilland-D-H-98-Mosquito-T-Mk-III.aspx.

ABOVE: FHCAM's "Wooden Wonder" makes its way across the sky during a SkyFair airshow.

ABOVE RIGHT: The lights below the Mosquito are recognition lights, colored red, amber, and green, and used for identification purposes. They were controlled in the cockpit and could relay Morse code signals or other coded messages, such as using a briefed color of the day to identify what type of aircraft was flying.

RIGHT: The Mosquito packed a deadly punch, with four of the machine guns on display off the nose. The cannons were underneath the nose.

During the FHCAM's Battle of Britain tribute, its Mosquito is seen with a Spitfire and Hurricane, the defenders of the British Empire against the Luftwaffe.

The belly of this Mosquito is painted black to help camouflage it during night missions.

Getting ready for a simulated attack run, *799* begins a shallow
dive, with six .50cal guns ready to go.

# CHAPTER 13
# CORSAIR

Nothing struck fear into the hearts of Japanese pilots quite like the Vought F4U Corsair, which achieved an 11:1 kill ratio and served both the US Navy and Marines in World War Two and Korea, as well as with the French in their southeast Asian conflicts. Designed as a carrier-based fighter-bomber, the Corsair became one of the most iconic aircraft in the Pacific, readily identified by its bent gull wings, which were used to accommodate the Corsair's large 13ft 4in propellers. The US Marine Corps made extensive use of the Corsair as a land-based close air support aircraft, able to carry 4,000lb of ordinance, while also able to clear the skies of enemy fighters, the latter type of mission being made famous by the VMF-214 "Black Sheep" and Major Gregory "Pappy" Boyington. Vought Aircraft originally received a contract to build the Corsair, designated as the F4U, and the US Navy gave additional follow-on contracts to Goodyear and Brewster, whose Corsairs were designated as FG and F3A, respectively. All Corsairs were powered by the Pratt & Whitney R-2800 engine, producing 2,400hp, which was also used by the F6F Hellcat and P-47 Thunderbolt. The Corsair was the first American single-engined aircraft to top 400mph, reaching speeds of up to 440mph with a range of 1,000 miles.

Although the Japanese Zero was the king of the Pacific skies at the beginning of the conflict, the Corsair was able to dethrone it, outperforming the Zero in nearly all aspects, except for slow-speed maneuverability, and it was able to hit hard with six .50cal machine guns. Better performance and tactics enabled Corsair pilots to dominate Japanese aircraft, with at least two Corsair pilots becoming an ace in a day: Major Pappy Boyington, and First Lieutenant Robert M. Hanson both shot down five aircraft over the Solomon Islands on September 16, 1943, and January 14, 1944, respectively. Just a couple of weeks later, Lieutenant Hanson again scored multiple victories, earning him the Medal of Honor, and his citation reads:

> Cut off from his division while deep in enemy territory during a high cover flight over Simpson Harbor on January 24, First Lieutenant Hanson waged a lone and gallant battle against hostile interceptors as they were orbiting to attack our bombers and, striking with devastating fury, brought down four Zeros and probably a fifth. Handling his plane superbly in both pursuit and attack measures, he was a master of individual air combat, accounting for a total of 25 Japanese aircraft in this theater of war.

Corsairs also proved invaluable in the Korean War, attacking ground targets, supporting C-47 supply drops, and even producing the US Navy's only ace of the war, with Lieutenant Guy Bordelon downing five enemy aircraft in 1952. The final Corsair was built in 1953 and delivered to the French Navy. The F4U lived on in the A-7 Corsair II, another carrier-based attack aircraft.

The Corsair featured here is owned and operated by the Planes of Fame Air Museum in Chino and is a combat veteran, serving with the Marine Corps in the south Pacific during Operation *Cartwheel*, which was the Allied operation to stop the Japanese from using Rabaul as a viable air base. It was originally built and delivered in 1943 and saw action with VMF-217 before being sold to MGM Studios as a movie prop after the war. Planes of Fame bought it in 1970 and restored it back to airworthiness in 1975, flying as *BuNo 17799* and becoming a Hollywood sensation, starring in *Baa Baa Blacksheep* and *Airwolf*, among other hit movies and TV shows. The Planes of Fame Corsair has its own webpage here: https://planesoffame.org/aircraft/plane-F4U-1A.

Another Corsair that has been expertly restored is the one flown by the Airbase Georgia Squadron of the CAF. Because of the high demand for the Corsair, Vought was unable to keep up with production, so the Goodyear company stepped in to help with manufacturing and their Corsairs were designated FG, and the CAF's Corsair is an FG-1D. It was one of the first aircraft in the CAF inventory, when it was bought in 1960 from private collectors who saved it from the scrapyard after it had been stricken from the Navy inventory in 1956. This FG-1D has been painted as *White 530*, representing the aircraft flown by Marine First Lieutenant M. O. Chance of VMF-312 who flew over Okinawa in 1945. More information about Lieutenant Chance's FG-1D Corsair is found at https://airbasegeorgia.org/fg-1d-corsair/.

With its magnificent two-tone blue US Navy scheme, the Planes of Fame Museum's Corsair, *799,* banks, speeding in towards the target area.

The famous landing gear of the Corsair is being retracted, with the inverted gull wing design used to accommodate the massive propellers.

**ABOVE LEFT:** Corsair *799* gets ready for its high-speed pass.

**ABOVE RIGHT:** After a successful attack mission, *799* pulls away and regroups for the next task.

**RIGHT:** The CAF's checkered *White 530* begins its airshow routine as it takes off and climbs to altitude.

The Corsair's distinctive shape and large engine can be seen as *White 530* banks.

*White 530* pulls away, giving a fantastic view of its glossy dark blue paint job.

In this wonderful topside view of the *White 530*, the CAF logo can be seen on the starboard side right in front of the pilot.

Although eventually replaced by more capable aircraft, the Wildcat proved that it could match the best the Imperial Japanese Navy had to offer.

# CHAPTER 14
# WILDCAT

Holding the line for the US Navy in the Pacific at the beginning of the war, the Grumman F4F Wildcat was the only carrier-based fighter that could even think about taking on the Japanese Zero. Thoroughly outclassed in nearly all aspects of performance, the heroic Wildcat pilots still fought off its superior opponents by using superior tactics and its heavier armor to its advantage. Wildcats were also used in the Battle of the Atlantic to help escort Allied shipping convoys, as well as during Operation *Torch* to take Morocco and Algeria from the Vichy French. The first Wildcat flew in 1937, began joining operational units by 1940 and ceased production by 1943 to make way for the F6F Hellcat; in this time, nearly 8,000 Wildcats were built. A single Pratt & Whitney R-1280 engine provided 1,200hp and gave the Wildcat a maximum speed of 330mph and a range of 850 miles. Four .50cal guns gave the Wildcat its teeth. The Wildcat could take an incredible amount of punishment with its heavy armor and self-sealing fuel tanks, a feature appreciated by its pilots, and its ruggedness impressed one of its most formidable opponents, Saburo Sakai, Japan's most famous ace, said:

> I had full confidence in my ability to destroy the Grumman and decided to finish off the enemy fighter with only my 7.7 mm machine guns. I turned the 20-mm cannon switch to the 'off' position, and closed in. For some strange reason, even after I had poured about five or six hundred rounds of ammunition directly into the Grumman, the airplane did not fall, but kept on flying. I thought this very odd—it had never happened before–and closed the distance between the two airplanes until I could almost reach out and touch the Grumman. To my surprise, the Grumman's rudder and tail were ripped to shreds, looking like an old torn piece of rag. With his plane in such condition, no wonder the enemy pilot was unable to continue fighting! (Sakai, p.216)

Another lifesaving innovation found in the Wildcat was the use of the ZB-1 homing beacon, which broadcast the location of a carrier within a 30-mile radius so that a lost or wounded Wildcat would be able to make it home.

The Corsair was not the only US Navy aircraft to produce an ace in a day. In January 1943, Marine Corps pilot First Lieutenant Jefferson DeBlanc led a flight of eight Wildcats, escorting 12 SBD Dauntless dive bombers attacking Japanese shipping. DeBlanc defended the SBDs during their attack and loitered afterwards to cover their withdrawal, downed two Mitsubishi F1M Petes and three Nakajima Ki-43 Oscars before he was shot down and baled out. After being rescued by a local tribe, he was traded back to the US Navy

**Medal of Honor recipient Captain Jefferson DeBlanc. (Photo courtesy of US Navy)**

for a bag of rice, and DeBlanc noted "most people cannot price out the exact amount of money they are worth, but I know exactly how much I am worth: one ten-pound sack of rice!" Lieutenant DeBlanc's heroics earned him the Medal of Honor. Although often overshadowed by more dominant Allied aircraft, the Wildcat played an important role in the Pacific by defending the fleet during the toughest days of the war, distinguishing themselves at the Battles of Coral Sea, Midway, and Guadalcanal.

The FM-2 Wildcat Sponsor Group in Upland, California, have paid tribute to the Wildcat by flying and maintaining N5833, which is currently painted with the squadron markings of VC-27, a composite squadron operating from the escort carrier USS *Savo Island* from 1943 to 1945 and seeing action in the Philippines. Squadron VC-27 shot down 61.5 enemy aircraft during the war, and its top ace was Lieutenant Ralph Elliott, Jr. N5833 originally was built by General Motors in August 1945 and was immediately sold as surplus, as the war was over before it could see action. It passed through the hands of numerous private owners until being donated to the CAF in the 1980s and certified for airworthiness in 1987. This Wildcat had also flown with an RAF livery from Squadron 835 from HMS *Nairana*. Wildcat N5833's website can be found at https://commemorativeairforce.org/units/93.

Lieutenant Ralph Elliott, Jr. is seen in the second row, eighth from the right, in this photo taken on December 2, 1944, with his squadron, VC-27. He was his squadron's top ace with nine kills. (Photo courtesy of the Department of the Navy, Office of Naval Records and Library)

For maximum camouflage, the Wildcat sported a tricolor livery, with white on the bottom, light blue in the middle, and dark blue on the top.

An early defender of the fleet, Wildcats had their hands full during the outset of World War Two. Fortunately, they were able to hold the line with their ruggedness and pilot skill.

Many pilots appreciated the tough armor plating behind them, protecting them from incoming enemy fire.

The Wildcat was an incredibly important participant in the Battle of Midway, protecting friendly bombers and defending the aircraft carriers from marauding Japanese aircraft.

*Minsi III* displays its 30 aerial victories, showing off the skill and prowess of the pilot.

# CHAPTER 15
# HELLCAT

Drawing on lessons learned from the Wildcat, and in an attempt to counter the Japanese Zero, Grumman Aircraft created the F6F Hellcat, which dominated the skies over the Pacific and became the US Navy's most prolific ace-maker, with no fewer than 300 Hellcat aces. The Hellcat design was influenced by the Navy's first World War Two ace and Medal of Honor recipient, Lieutenant Commander Edward O'Hare, who provided feedback to Grumman engineers on the limitations of the Wildcat and how the Zero could be defeated. Improved visibility and flight controls made the Hellcat easier to land on a carrier than the Corsair, and its ruggedness helped pilots survive enemy encounters, with over 200lb of armor plating around the cockpit and oil tanks. Like the Corsair and Thunderbolt, the Hellcat had a Pratt & Whitney R-2800 engine with 2000hp, giving it a maximum speed of nearly 400mph and a combat range of 1,000 miles. It had six .50cal machine guns and could carry up to 4,000lb of bombs, making it lethal against air and ground targets. The Hellcat's success is evident in the number produced: over 12,000 aircraft rolled off the assembly lines in under three years, owing not only to its combat effectiveness but also good systems design, which helped streamline manufacturing. Although later versions of the Hellcat were fitted with radar equipment to aid with night fighting, it was eventually eclipsed by the upgraded F8F Bearcat. The Hellcat was removed from frontline duty and relegated to training and drone missions but distinguished itself as the first aircraft type to fly for the Blue Angels, the US Navy's flight demonstration team.

The performance and toughness of the Hellcat are legendary, and, paired with superior pilots, it proved nearly unstoppable. Captain David McCampbell is the US Navy's all-time leading ace, with 34 aerial victories while flying the Hellcat, all while earning a Medal of Honor. On October 24, 1944, McCampbell shot down nine enemy aircraft during the Battle of Leyte Gulf: "Fighting desperately but with superb skill against such overwhelming airpower, he shot down nine Japanese planes and, completely disorganizing the enemy group, forced the remainder to abandon the attack before a single aircraft could reach the Fleet." Hellcats were instrumental in the lopsided American victory during the Battle of the Philippine Sea, known to American aviators as the "Great Marianas Turkey Shoot" in 1944, which

Commander (later Captain) David McCambell poses in the cockpit of his F6F Hellcat *Minsi III* on board USS *Essex* (CV-9), circa early October 1944. Note 21 kills marked on the aircraft, the number credited to Commander McCampbell as of this time. (Photo courtesy of US Navy)

resulted in about 20 lost Hellcats to over 400 Japanese aircraft of all types and two Japanese fleet carriers sunk. In a concatenation of favorable events for the US Navy, the Hellcats and their fellow naval aviators struck a decisive blow against the Japanese, effectively ending Japanese carrier operations for the rest of the war.

Paying homage to Captain McCampbell is the SoCal Wing of the CAF, with its F6F-5 Hellcat painted as *Minsi III*. Originally a Frankenstein-esque aircraft, this Hellcat was built with parts from different F6F variants as well as from a Corsair. After the war, it was abandoned and rediscovered in bad condition at the Fergus Falls Municipal Airport,

and it was sold to the CAF in 1970 after some initial renovations. In 1986, it went through a massive and true renovation process that took over a decade to finish, with corrosion and general wear slowing progress significantly. With additional funding and manpower, *Minsi III* was finally finished in 1995, ready to grace the skies once again. Nearly a complete rebuild, *Minsi III* serves as a reminder to the history of the veterans who flew the aircraft and those volunteers and members of the CAF who work tirelessly and donate money to keep these warbirds flying. Additional information about *Minsi III* can be found here: https://www.cafsocal.com/our-aircrafts/our-aircraft-and-history/gruman-f6f-hellcat/.

This bottom view highlights the six .50cal machine guns mounted in the wings, which were responsible for downing so many enemy aircraft.

The white stripe on the tail indicates that this aircraft belonged to the Commander, Air Group (CAG) pilot, making him responsible for the upcoming air battle.

A rare sight of a Hellcat flying in formation with a Mustang, representing two of the most dominant fighters in the war.

The Hellcat flies with its scheduled replacement, the Bearcat. Although the Bearcat was too late to see action, it was slated to be the dominant aircraft in the Pacific.

Although too late to see combat in World War Two, it is obvious that this Bearcat would have continued the Navy's domination, thanks to its hard-hitting cannons and powerful engine.

# CHAPTER 16
# BEARCAT

Grumman's attempt to make the ultimate carrier-based propeller aircraft culminated with the F8F Bearcat, but this aircraft missed major action when World War Two ended and the Korean War saw the advent of high-performance jets. The Bearcat was able to outperform its predecessor, the Hellcat, because of a significant decrease in weight, while using the same Pratt & Whitney R-2800 engine, resulting in a higher climb rate and top speed of 450mph. It also sported the US Navy's first bubble canopy for greater visibility and reduced weight. Only 1,200 were built, and further orders were canceled when the F9F Panther and F2H Banshee entered service. The Bearcat saw some service in southeast Asia with the French Air Force and performed for the Blue Angels but mostly sat on the sidelines, an unfortunate fate for such a high-performance aircraft. It was designed to carry four 20mm cannons and up to 1,000lb worth of bombs, which would make it an extremely heavy hitter, especially in the air-to-air role. Because of its speed and climb rate, the Bearcat has become popular among air racers, breaking and holding speed records for piston-powered aircraft. Although unable to significantly contribute to the war effort, the Bearcat has found a home with private collectors and racers, making sure its legacy still lives on.

The SoCal Wing of the CAF flies the beautiful Wildcat *BuNo 122674*, painted as it would have looked when it served in the US Navy. Originally constructed as an F8F-2P, this example was delivered to the Navy in 1949 as a photo reconnaissance aircraft and sold to a private owner in 1958. No fewer than six owners handled this magnificent aircraft before the CAF took possession in 1972, and it was flown hard until 1989 when it underwent a significant restoration with nearly all internal fuel lines, electrical, and hydraulic parts being completely replaced. Retaining its high-performance characteristics, *BuNo 122674* continually wows audiences at airshows nationwide. More information on *BuNo 122674* can be found here https://www.cafsocal.com/our-aircrafts/our-aircraft-and-history/gruman-f8f-2-bearcat/.

The Bearcat improved on an already-dominant Hellcat and would have most likely been the plane to beat in the Pacific.

Cats on the prowl! A Hellcat and Bearcat form up as they look for prey.

*White 14* powers through the Southern Californian air, mesmerizing with its spiral nose, letting the ground crew know the propellers are spinning.

# CHAPTER 17
# FW 190

One of the most feared and successful fighters for the Axis powers was the Focke-Wulf Fw 190 Würger (Shrike), which proved to be the bane of the US Eighth Air Force over Europe. Able to accomplish a variety of missions, the Fw 190 could carry a large payload, making it suitable for air-to-ground missions whilst being able to hold its own against top-of-the-line fighters such as the Spitfire. Along with the Messerschmitt Bf 109, the Fw 190 packed a powerful one-two punch on both Western and Eastern Fronts. It had excellent maneuverability and firepower, making it a favorite of many Luftwaffe pilots. Designed specifically with combat in mind, the Focke-Wulf designers made it as pilot-friendly as possible, instead of trying to brute-force speed and firepower into the aircraft. As a result, the flight controls were easier to handle, and the pilot workload was reduced. Although easier to fly than its contemporaries, the Fw 190 was no slouch when it came to combat effectiveness, as it had a top speed of more than 400mph over a 600-mile range. It could take down any enemy aircraft with its four 20mm cannons and two 13mm machine guns. The reliable BMW 801 engine that provided 1,600hp, was also used in the Junkers Ju 88 medium bomber. Over 20,000 examples were built for the Luftwaffe between 1941 and 1945, and it saw action in all theaters including North Africa and the final Defense of the Reich.

The Fw 190 produced many of the top aces in the history of aerial combat. Legends like Otto Kittel and Walter Nowotny scored over 250 victories each, predominantly on the Eastern Front, with many of their kills in the Fw 190. Another important role it filled was to defend against heavy bomber attacks, with some variants outfitted with 30mm cannons that could shred B-17 Flying Fortresses, and although less maneuverable and requiring an escort, these upgraded Fw 190s proved extremely effective. Because of its speed and large payload, the Fw 190 was a natural choice for conversion to a fighter-bomber and was used extensively on the Eastern Front, where target-rich environments led to high tallies of ground kills. On one occasion, an Fw 190 was even able to sink a British submarine in the Mediterranean Sea.

Oskar Bosch was a famous Fw 190 pilot who shot down at least eight heavy bombers over Europe and had a total of 18 victories. He flew an Fw 190 named *White 14* and is honored by the Planes of Fame Air Museum with a replica Fw 190A-8/N built by Flug Werk, using original blueprints and some casting dies as well. The Flug Werk version was built in Romania in 2000 and was bought by a private collector and used in various air races using a Pratt & Whitney R-2800 engine. In 2018, Planes of Fame bought *White 14,* and it has since been flying in the Planes of Fame airshow in Chino, wowing American audiences who rarely get to see Axis aircraft. More information about *White 14* can be found at https://planesoffame.org/aircraft/plane-190A-9.

Ready for takeoff! *White 14* gets ready to thrill audiences at the Planes of Fame Museum.

After another outstanding performance, *White 14* takes a well-deserved break and rests on the tarmac.

Seeing the Fw 190 in the air is a real treat, as it is one of the rarest warbirds in the US.

Although outmatched by top-of-the-line Luftwaffe aircraft, the Hurricane still played an extremely important role in the Battle of Britain.

# CHAPTER 18
# HURRICANE

Although often overshadowed by the Supermarine Spitfire during the Battle of Britain, the Hawker Hurricane proved a valiant stalworth in the defense of Britain, being responsible for over 60 percent of Luftwaffe losses during the 1940 air battle. Originally armed with eight .303cal machine guns, the Hurricane could throw a lot of lead downrange, and its firepower was appreciated by Allied forces in all theaters in World War Two. The Hurricane wings were made of fabric, making it lighter and easy to manufacture and bridge the gap between biplanes and the all-metallic Spitfire. It was Britain's first monoplane fighter. Equipped with the Rolls-Royce Merlin XX engine, the Hurricane could reach a top speed of 340mph with a range of 600 miles. Sometimes scorned for being outdated, the Hurricane served through the entirety of the war with its ease of flight and maintenance, and it silenced its critics with its performance against its enemies. All told, over 14,000 Hurricanes were built for the UK, Australia, Canada, the Soviet Union, and other Allied air forces. Hurricanes were also used in a limited night fighter role and would occasionally jump bombers taking off or landing from German-controlled airfields in France at night.

During the Battle of Britain, the Hurricane was typically used to attack bomber formations while the escorting Spitfires kept the Bf 109s at bay. This was due to the Hurricane's ability to be a steady firing platform for its eight machine guns, and the fact that the Bf 109 could defeat the Hurricane in a dogfight during most engagements, although at lower altitudes the Hurricane had the advantage in a turn fight. This powerful tandem between Hurricanes and Spitfires resulted in the downing of over 800 German bombers, sparing countless civilians and helping stop Operation *Seelöwe* (*Sea Lion*), the German plan to invade Britain. The only Victoria Cross awarded during the Battle of Britain went to Hurricane pilot Flight Lieutenant Eric Nicolson:

> During an engagement with the enemy near Southampton on 16th August 1940, Flight Lieutenant Nicolson's aircraft was hit by four cannon shells, two of which wounded him whilst another set fire to the gravity tank. When about to abandon his aircraft owing to flames in the cockpit he sighted an enemy fighter. This he attacked and shot down, although as a result of staying in his burning aircraft he sustained serious burns to his hands, face, neck and legs.

Another legendary Hurricane pilot was Squadron Leader Marmaduke "Pat" Pattle, who shot down 50 enemy aircraft, 35 of them in a Hurricane, and gave his life during the Battle of Greece. Elsewhere, the Hurricane served the British Empire with distinction, particularly during the Siege of Malta, where it held off the Italian and German Air Forces, ensuring vital supply lines through the Mediterranean were kept open for the Allies.

There are fewer than 20 flying Hurricanes in the world, and one of them resides at the FHCAM, which was originally slated to become a Sea Hurricane, tasked to protect convoys in the Atlantic. It was delivered to the RCAF by the Canadian Car and Foundry company in 1942 but never saw action and was converted to a Mk.XIIA model. It was involved in a crash in Ontario and subsequently abandoned by the RCAF and later rediscovered and restored to airworthiness in 2007. It currently displays the markings *Z5429*, representing the RCAF 135 Squadron known as the "Bulldogs," assigned for home defense. More history about *Z5429* can be found at http://flyingheritage.org/Explore/The-Collection/Britain/Hawker-Hurricane-Mk-XIIA.aspx.

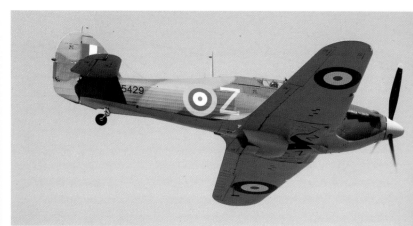

The cowling on the belly of the Hurricane is a radiator scoop, which serves to cool the engine. During a water landing, it would fill quickly so the pilot had to get out immediately to avoid going down with the aircraft.

ABOVE: Hurricane *Z5429* takes to the skies, ready to deal out damage with its eight machine guns.

RIGHT: Hurricanes were constantly attacking Luftwaffe bombers, shooting down much of the heavy aircraft during the Battle of Britain.

In this fantastic Battle of Britain tribute, the Hurricane is seen trailing a Mosquito and Spitfire.

The "Bulldogs" logo is displayed on the nose as Hurricane *Z5429* taxis back to the hangar after a great show.

Nicknamed "The Fork-Tailed Devil," the Lightning has an unmistakable silhouette that struck fear into the hearts of its enemies.

# CHAPTER 19
# LIGHTNING

The designers at Lockheed must have been thrilled when they heard that the Luftwaffe gave their P-38 Lightning the nickname "The Fork-Tailed Devil" ("der Gabelschwanz-Teufel"), validating their work in creating a powerhouse of a fighter, interceptor, and ground-attack aircraft. With its speed, range, and firepower, the Lightning was most deadly doing long-range fighter sweeps, clearing the way for heavy bombers in Europe to strike deep into enemy territory. Time and time again, the agility of the Lightning surprised its opponents, who could not believe such a large aircraft could be so maneuverable. The twin-engined, boom-tailed design was radical for its time, enabling a larger fuel load, giving it a range of 1,300 miles and a blazing fast speed of over 400mph. Two Allison V-1710 engines put out 1,600hp each and powered counter-rotating propellers. Because the engines were on either side of the cockpit nacelle, its four .50cal machine guns and single 20mm cannon were mounted in front of the pilot, reducing dispersion issues caused with wing-mounted guns. At the outset of the war, the P-38 was one of the few viable USAAF fighters that would be able to compete with the Bf 109 and Japanese Zero, making it an invaluable part of the early Allied defense. Able to escort bombers to Germany and back, the Lightning defended the heavies until the P-51 Mustang was able to be fielded in large numbers, helping to make daylight bombing raids viable throughout 1943 and 1944. Towards the end of the war, as the P-51 took over the escort role, Lightning pilots also distinguished themselves in the fighter-bomber role, able to carry heavy bombs and rockets and attack enemy supply lines, vehicles, and positions. Over 10,000 Lightnings were produced during the war but were subsequently retired in 1949, made obsolete by the jet age. Although the Mustang eventually outshined the Lightning, the P-38 proved to be one of the most valuable multirole and innovative aircraft in aviation history.

The Lightning's combat effectiveness was proven by Major Richard Bong, who was America's top ace with 40 total kills, all in the P-38. He was awarded the Medal of Honor for being "voluntarily and at his own urgent request engaged in repeated combat missions, including unusually hazardous sorties over Balikpapan, Borneo, and in the Leyte

*23 Skidoo* flaunts its nose art and nine aerial victories over Japanese aircraft.

area of the Philippines. His aggressiveness and daring resulted in his shooting down 8 enemy airplanes during this period." One of the most famous Lightning missions was the shootdown of Japanese Admiral Isoroku Yamamoto on April 18, 1943. Sixteen P-38s received intelligence that Yamamoto would be transported to Bouganville, and they traveled 600 miles to intercept two G4M Bettys and six A6M Zeros. Both Bettys and one Zero were shot down, and Yamamoto was killed during the attack compared to the loss of one P-38. This raid boosted American morale and deprived the Japanese Navy of one of its best strategists. The legacy of the P-38 is carried on by the latest fighter in the American inventory: the F-35 Lightning II. Like the P-38, the F-35 is a multirole aircraft that has radical new aircraft designs including stealth, vertical/short takeoff and landing capabilities, and advanced electronics.

There are fewer than a dozen airworthy Lightnings left, and the Planes of Fame Air Museum flies one of them, painted as *23 Skidoo*, which was flown by Captain Perry Dahl of the 432nd Fighter Squadron. Dahl was a noted ace, shooting down nine enemy aircraft and receiving the Silver Star for defending a flight from an ambush. The original P-38 airframe that currently carries the *23 Skidoo* colors started out as a trainer in California and was transferred to an aeronautics school to help instruct prospective maintenance crew. In 1959, the Planes of Fame bought it and was able to restore it to flight status in 1988; it has since become a sought-after photography subject. Its silhouette is as unmistakable today as it was when it first saw combat and continues to amaze those who are fortunate enough to see it in the air. The Planes of Fame P-38 website is https://planesoffame.org/aircraft/plane-P-38J.

*23 Skidoo* gets ready for a simulated attack run, showcasing its multirole capabilities, able to perform long range escort, intercept, and close air support.

Combining speed, range, maneuverability, and firepower, the Lightning was able to accomplish any mission asked of it.

The air inlet made the P-40 a natural canvas for the famous shark mouth, striking fear in opposing Japanese pilots and providing a symbol of hope and resistance to the Chinese and American public.

# CHAPTER 20
# WARHAWK

The shark mouth livery on the nose of the Curtiss P-40 Warhawk was the icon of early American fighting prowess in East Asia, representing the American Volunteer Group, which fought on behalf of the Republic of China during the beginning of the war. Warhawks served primarily with the USAAF, RAF, RCAF, and Royal Australian Air Force and in the North African and East Asian theaters at lower altitudes, partially because they were outmatched by Luftwaffe aircraft when flying above 15,000 feet. Rapid production and good performance made the Warhawk the third most produced Allied fighter of the war, with over 13,500 built in all. The P-40 was powered by an Allison V-1710 engine that produced 1,240hp, a top speed of 330mph and a range of about 700 miles. Armed with six .50cal machine guns and up to 2,000lb of bombs, the P-40 was able to shred through its lightly armored Japanese opponents.

Unable to outturn the Zero, P-40 pilots adopted "boom and zoom" tactics, slashing through enemy formations from a higher altitude and zoom-climbing back up to regain energy. As described by Brigadier General Claire Chennault, Commander of the Flying Tigers, "Never stay in and fight; never try to turn; never try to mix with them, get altitude and dive on them and keep going, never lose speed or take for granted that the planes you could see were all there because we would always be outnumbered" (Bird p.126, Chennault). With the Flying Tigers, this resulted in an extremely favorable kill ratio of 7.5:1, a remarkable record considering that they were outnumbered in nearly all engagements. The Flying Tigers produced no fewer than 19 aces, with several legendary

pilots among them, including Pappy Boyington, who has been mentioned earlier in this book, and Tex Hill, who shot down 18 enemy aircraft and would end his career as a brigadier general.

During the surprise attack on Pearl Harbor on December 7, 1941, two P-40s were able to get airborne to defend their base. Second Lieutenants Kenneth Taylor and George Welch took off in their Warhawks under heavy fire and fended off attacks by D3A Val dive bombers, and although they were outnumbered 6:1, they managed to shoot down two Vals and damage at least one other, and fought until they ran out of ammunition. They landed to rearm and return to the fight but were ordered to stay on the ground by superior officers; however, they promptly ignored the orders, with Welch reportedly saying, "to hell with that" and continued back into the fight. Contending with both enemy aircraft and friendly anti-aircraft fire, Taylor and Welch shot down an additional two enemy aircraft, one Val and one Zero, and damaging at least one other aircraft. They continued to chase away enemy aircraft until they ran out of ammunition. Taylor was wounded in the arm and received the Purple Heart, and both men were awarded the Distinguished Flying Cross (they were denied the Medal of Honor because they disobeyed orders to stay on the ground). Their efforts in the face of overwhelming odds drove Japanese aircraft away from Haleiwa Airfield, saving their fellow soldiers and vital infrastructure.

The FHCAM has beautifully restored a P-40C that has since been painted to represent the Flying Tigers. This example is a combat veteran built in the United States and sold to the RAF, which promptly gave it to the Soviet Union in 1941. From there, it flew over Murmansk against German forces, where it received many bullet holes from small-caliber weapons, all but one of which were patched up by Soviet maintenance crews. It was shot in the oil tank and was forced to belly land in 1942, after which it was abandoned and stricken near Murmansk. It was recovered underwater in Lake Kod Ozero in 1997 and eventually shipped to Chino for restoration in 1998. A year later, the FHCAM took possession of the P-40 and has been flying it ever since under Flying Tigers colors. More information about this Flying Tiger is found at http://flyingheritage.org/Explore/The-Collection/United-States/Curtiss-P-40C-Tomahawk.aspx.

**The Flying Tigers' logo was designed by the Walt Disney company, giving an additional mystique to the American Volunteer Group.**

Flying under Republic of China colors, the American Volunteer Group was given the nickname "Flying Tigers," a Chinese colloquialism for a doubly powerful entity, as a tiger could increase its ferociousness even more by being able to fly. Inspiring awe in friends and terror into enemies, the viciousness of the Flying Tigers became the stuff of legends.

Affectionately known as the "Jug," the rotund shape of the P-47 looked like a milk jug of the day. The name also alluded to its heavy weight and payload.

# CHAPTER 21
# THUNDERBOLT

One of the toughest and hardest-hitting fighter aircraft in World War Two was the Republic P-47 Thunderbolt, with its eight .50cal machine guns and 2,500lb payload, it was able to withstand intense punishment and still make it home. Unparalleled as a fighter-bomber, the Thunderbolt was also surprisingly maneuverable, able to compete in a dogfight with any of its contemporary enemies. At 10,000lb when empty, the Thunderbolt was one of the heaviest fighters of the war and used its weight to out-dive its opponents to escape while regaining energy to reposition for an attack. Although diving to gain speed was a useful tactic, the P-47 was plenty fast in straight-and-level flight, topping out at over 420mph, powered by the legendary Pratt & Whitney R-2800 engine. The Thunderbolt's Achilles' heel was its range, as it was unable to escort heavy bombers from England to Berlin and back, and this escort duty eventually was ceded to the Mustang. The Thunderbolt shot down over 7,000 aircraft of all types and played a pivotal role in both European and Pacific theaters. It also dropped over 130,000 tons of bombs in support of ground forces in the close air support role, making the Thunderbolt lethal in the air and on the ground. Over 15,500 Thunderbolts were built, serving the USAF until 1947, and although they have long since been retired, the legendary toughness and air-to-ground capabilities live on with the A-10 Thunderbolt II.

One of the most famous fighter groups in all aerial warfare was the 56th Fighter Group, known as the "Wolfpack," commanded by Colonel Hubert "Hub" Zemke. The Wolfpack flew the P-47, and under Zemke's leadership, tactics were implemented to take advantage of its strength in a dive while not engaging in battles that required quick acceleration. As a result, the Wolfpack racked up 665 aerial victories between June 1943 and April 1945, with Lieutenant Colonel Francis Gabreski and Major Robert Johnson leading the pack with 28 and 27 kills, respectively. However, Johnson might not have been able to achieve his quintuple-ace status were it not for the durability of the Thunderbolt. On June 26, 1943, Johnson found himself in dire straits after being ambushed by 16 Fw 190s en route to an escort mission. In the initial salvo, Johnson's P-47 took 21 20mm shells, thus destroying his hydraulic systems and catching fire. The canopy jammed, and Johnson was unable to bale out while his aircraft entered an out-of-control spin. Johnson was able to recover from the spin, and the fire extinguished itself, but he was not out of the woods yet. Another Fw 190, flown by Major Egon Mayer, began spraying the Thunderbolt with hundreds of 7.92mm rounds, but Johnson was unable to fight back because his guns were jammed. Maneuvering violently and using his aircraft's toughness, Johnson simply outlasted Mayer, who eventually ran out of ammunition and returned home. There were over 200 bullet holes throughout the aircraft, and despite shrapnel wounds and minor burns, Johnson returned to the fight just five days later, owing his life to the ruggedness of the Thunderbolt.

Honoring one of Seattle's own, the FHCAM has wonderfully restored a P-47D Thunderbolt to honor Colonel Ralph Jenkins and his *Tallahassee Lassie*. This P-47 was originally built in 1945 but only flew for the National Guard, where it was transferred to the Brazilian Air Force in the 1950s. The Thunderbolt eventually made its way to the FHCAM in 1998, where it was repainted and refurbished as *Tallahassee Lassie*. Jenkins flew his P-47 in Europe, where he participated in 129 missions, including flying air combat patrols on D-Day. He asked his squadron painter to decorate his aircraft with his then-girlfriend and later wife, Tiero, who was from Tallahassee, Florida, for good luck and inspiration. Both his aircraft and wife proved to be faithful, as he was brought back down to Earth safely on multiple occasions by both of them. Jenkins and his wife were able to see Tallahassee Lassie fly again in 2009 when they were guests of honor at the FHCAM's inaugural SkyFair airshow. The history of *Tallahassee Lassie* can be found here http://flyingheritage.org/Explore/The-Collection/United-States/Republic-P-47D-Thunderbolt.aspx

**ABOVE RIGHT:** The P-47 could take damage as well as it could dish it out, being able to sustain heavy enemy fire and bring the pilot home.

**BELOW LEFT:** With eight .50cal machine guns and the ability to carry a combination of bombs and rockets, the Thunderbolt proved to be a highly effective ground-attack aircraft.

**BELOW RIGHT:** The FHCAM has restored *Tallahassee Lassie* beautifully, making sure its silver livery continues to shine brightly.

ABOVE LEFT: *Tallahassee Lassie* and *Upupa epops* fly in formation. Both helped provide escort to heavy USAAF bombers over Europe.

ABOVE RIGHT: This underside view of *Tallahassee Lassie* shows the bomb and rocket racks, which were able to carry ten HVAR rockets and 2,500lb of bombs.

RIGHT: Another great formation features *Tallahassee Lassie* flying the "Tail-End Charlie" of a formation consisting of a Mosquito, Spitfire, Hurricane, and Mustang.

Arguably the most famous fighter of all time, the Mustang has earned all its accolades by changing the course of the war, enabling strategic bombing to continue into the heart of the Reich.

# CHAPTER 22
# MUSTANG

Often seen as the apotheosis of aircraft design throughout all of aviation history, the North American P-51 Mustang changed the course of World War Two by escorting heavy bombers from England to Germany and back while being able to outperform nearly any aircraft the Axis powers could throw at it. The history and performance of the Mustang is extremely well documented, and deservedly so, as it kept the Allies in the fight and eventually pushed them to victory. For an authoritative look at the development of the P-51, look no further than Key Publishing's *Mustang: The Untold Story* by Matthew Willis. Suffice to say, even at the outset of its production, the Mustang was an incredible aircraft, taking its first flight just 102 days after the contract for design was signed. Serving in all corners of the globe for the Allies, the Mustang combined top-tier speed, maneuverability, and range in order to engage and defeat challengers in Europe and the Pacific. The D-model of the Mustang had a top speed of 440mph and a range of over 1,600 miles with external drop tanks while carrying six .50cal machine guns and up to 1,000lb of bombs. After World War Two, the P-51 was rebranded as the F-51 and served as a fighter-bomber in Korea, and although vulnerable to ground fire, its long range once again proved invaluable, as it was able to reach targets in North Korea while taking off from Japan. In total, over 15,000 Mustangs were built, highlighting its popularity among Allied forces. Its high performance and legendary status have led it to become a popular choice among private aviation racers and collectors while also serving with air forces worldwide, including the Dominican Air Force until 1984!

When the Mustang's performance was combined with expert flying, the P-51 was invincible. One such pilot who could not be stopped was Lieutenant Colonel James Howard, who, in the words of General Robert Travis, flew "against what seemed to be the entire Luftwaffe." Howard was awarded the Medal of Honor for his actions in his P-51 on January 11, 1944:

> [W]ith his group, [Howard] at once engaged the enemy and himself destroyed a German ME. 110. As a result of this attack Col. Howard lost contact with his group, and at once returned to the level of the bomber formation. He then saw that the bombers were being heavily attacked by enemy airplanes and that no other friendly fighters were at hand. While Col. Howard could have waited to attempt to assemble his group before engaging the enemy, he chose instead to attack single-handed a formation of more than 30 German airplanes. With utter disregard for his own safety he immediately pressed home determined attacks for some 30 minutes, during which time he destroyed 3 enemy airplanes and probably destroyed and damaged others. Toward the end of this engagement 3 of his guns went out of action and his fuel supply was becoming dangerously low. Despite these handicaps and the almost insuperable odds against him, Col. Howard continued his aggressive action in an attempt to protect the bombers from the numerous fighters.

Another groundbreaking group of pilots who flew the Mustang included the Tuskegee Airmen, who fought against both racial discrimination and Axis pilots. Their primary mission was to escort bombers into Germany, and most reports indicate that none of the bombers was lost due to enemy fire; a testament to their skill, bravery, and aircraft.

Because of its popularity with collectors, looking for Mustangs to photograph is usually fruitful, and owners range from ordinary citizens to museums to movie stars. *Lady Alice* is an example of a Mustang operated by a single person, Dr. Kendall Wagner. It was built in 1945 and sold to a private owner in 1963 in Hawaii, where it flew until 1972 when it was damaged during a landing and was sent to California for repairs. It became airworthy again and flew about once a year during airshows. In 2006, Dr. Wagner purchased *Lady Alice*, and he personally pilots the Mustang at airshows in his own time. Another airshow veteran is *Gunfighter*, which also rolled off the factory floor in 1945 and had a brief stint in Europe before returning home to the Air National Guard. *Gunfighter* was sold as surplus in 1956 and somehow ended up in El Salvador, flying for the Salvadoran Air Force against Honduras in the so-called "Football War" in 1973. It made its way back to the US under the care of the CAF in 1977 and has since been repainted in *Gunfighter* colors and has flown regularly for over 40 years. One more great organization that restores aircraft is the Southern Heritage Air Foundation (SHAF), and its Mustang, *Charlotte's Chariot II*, pays homage to Lieutenant Colonel Cary Salter, who received a Distinguished Flying Cross and Silver Star for his actions over Europe in 1944. The original Mustang was built in 1944 and sold to a private collector in 1957, bouncing around many different owners until 2010 when SHAF took possession and repainted it in the *Charlotte's Chariot II* livery. Its bright paint scheme and unique "pi" identification number make it the star of any airshow. Not to be outdone by the other awesome groups, the FHCAM has a Mustang of its own, painted as *Upupa epops*, named after

an awkward and cantankerous bird; an ironic name given to a graceful and speedy fighter. A rarity among restored aircraft, *Upupa epops* has been restored as it was when it originally served in World War Two with the 353rd Fighter Group over Europe, flown by Captain Harrison Tordoff, who even shot down an ME-262 in this Mustang. From there, it served in the Royal Swedish Air Force and then in the Dominican Republic Air Force. In 1998, the FHCAM acquired the Mustang and restored it almost perfectly to its original 1945 state. Tordoff was reunited with his aircraft in 2003, providing validation for the hard work put forth by the staff at the FHCAM.

The P-51D, represented here by *Lady Alice,* is the definitive version of the Mustang, with its signature bubble canopy.

**ABOVE LEFT:** The Mustang was indeed a great *Gunfighter*, with its six .50cal machine guns shredding enemy targets in the air and on the ground.

**ABOVE RIGHT:** Nothing brought more relief to USAAF bomber formations than seeing the silver glint of escorting Mustangs.

**RIGHT:** When fitted with the Rolls Royce Merlin engine, the P-51 was able to dominate the skies over Europe and the Pacific.

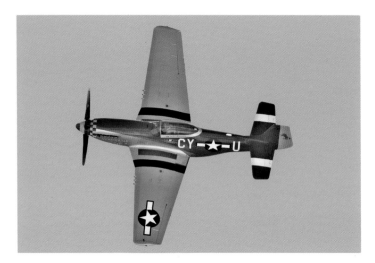

**ABOVE LEFT:** The beautiful silhouette of *Gunfighter* is on full display in this top view.

**ABOVE RIGHT:** Larry Lumpkin is the primary sponsor of *Gunfighter* and has over 1,200 hours in the P-51. He has flown *Gunfighter* for over 18 years.

**LEFT:** *Gunfighter* banks away from the audience, giving an excellent view of its flaps.

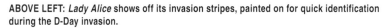

**ABOVE LEFT:** *Lady Alice* shows off its invasion stripes, painted on for quick identification during the D-Day invasion.

**ABOVE RIGHT:** Mustangs and the rest of the USAAF had established air supremacy so completely that they were more concerned about friendly anti-aircraft fire than being identified by the enemy, forgoing any attempt at camouflage.

**RIGHT:** *Upupa epops* climbs up after takeoff and begins its awesome aerobatic routine.

**ABOVE LEFT:** The beautiful yellow and black checkered nose makes quite an impression and stands out among nose art designs.

**ABOVE RIGHT:** The chrome silver of *Upupa epops* is meticulously maintained by the devoted volunteers of the FHCAM.

**LEFT:** *Upupa epops* escorts a Mosquito across the skies over the FHCAM.

From right to left, a rare formation of a Mosquito, Spitfire, Thunderbolt, and Mustang can be seen thundering in the heavens.

Among many of the unique features of the King Cobra is the
top-mounted air intake for the carburetor, aft of the canopy.

# CHAPTER 23

# KING COBRA

Based on the lackluster P-39 Airacobra, the Bell P-63 King Cobra looked to make up for its predecessor's deficiencies, most notably its high-altitude performance, which had been inhibited by a lack of turbocharger. Although rejected by the RAF and USAAF for combat use, the P-63 attracted interest from the Soviet Air Force which had already been using the P-39 extensively and to great effect and was looking for a familiar upgrade to its Airacobras. Like the P-39, the P-63 had an unusual mid-body engine mounting, which was designed to free up space in the nose to mount a heavy 37mm cannon through the propeller hub, and had a secondary advantage in streamlining the nose profile for better aerodynamic efficiency. In addition to the massive cannon in the nose, the P-63 carried four .50cal machine guns and had a payload of up to 1,500lb of bombs. It was powered by an Allison V-1710, which gave the King Cobra 1,800hp and a maximum speed of 410mph. It did not have great range, but that disadvantage proved to be negligible on the Eastern Front as missions were short and flown at low levels. Over 3,000 King Cobras were built, fighting almost exclusively for the Soviets. Although the 37mm cannon would lead many observers to believe the P-63 was used exclusively as a ground attack aircraft, it also saw extensive action against the Luftwaffe, and although exact numbers are not known due to records manipulation, the King Cobra performed well against its German counterparts. Along with the P-39, the P-63 proved to be one of the most successful fixed-wing aircraft Bell produced. It continued on with the Soviet Air Force until 1953, with the NATO reporting name *Fred*.

Due to the sleek airframe resulting from the engine being mounted behind the cockpit, the P-63 has good aerodynamic qualities and has become a popular racing aircraft among private pilots. One such aircraft is owned by the CAF, restored with the serial number 311719. It was originally constructed in 1943 but had less than 25 hours of flight time with the USAAF, eventually being sold to a private collector in 1946 and competing in many races until 1981, when it was transferred to the CAF. During its time as a racer, its best finish was fourth place in the National Championship Air Races in 1978, proving that it was a fast aircraft, even if it was no longer in its prime. The CAF repainted it in Soviet livery until 1995, when it was restored to its original USAAF silver paint scheme. In the early 2010s, 311719 underwent a serious overhaul, and it is currently based in Midland, flying for the CAF Airpower Museum. Additional information about the King Cobra can be found at https://commemorativeairforce.org/aircraft/26.

The mid-engine mounting also pushed the exhaust behind the pilot. The overall effect was a streamlined nose and a trickier job for the maintenance crew.

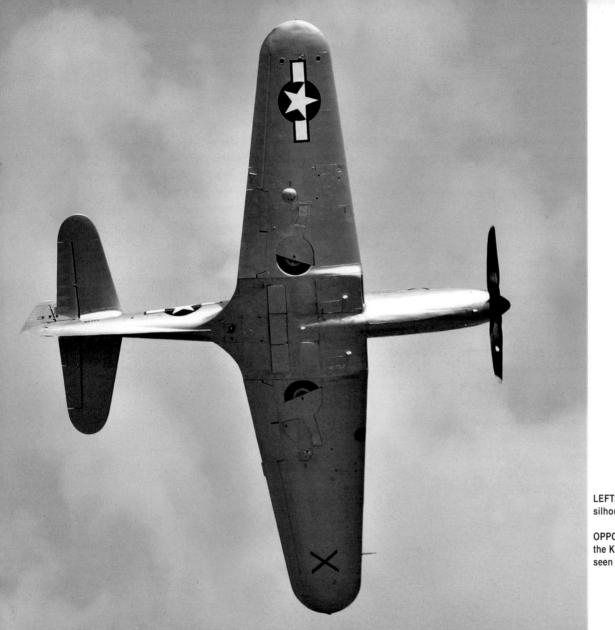

LEFT: This underside shot gives a great view of the silhouette of the King Cobra.

OPPOSITE: Able to do battle with any Luftwaffe fighter, the King Cobra possessed great maneuverability, as seen here.

A happy and enthusiastic passenger mans the rear guns; a reminder that the CAF offers rides on the Dauntless.

# CHAPTER 24
# DAUNTLESS

An early stalwart in the fight against the Imperial Japanese Navy in the Pacific, the Douglas SBD Dauntless dive-bomber was the preeminent carrier-killer for the US Navy, responsible for sinking six Japanese carriers. The Dauntless also sank more enemy shipping than any other aircraft in the war and provided valuable close air support to ground units during amphibious landings in both the Pacific and the Mediterranean. It had great range, durability, armament, and dive control, making it a favorite among pilots, even if it was not as maneuverable or as fast as other aircraft. Overall, nearly 6,000 Dauntless dive bombers were built for both the US Navy and USAAF. Plodding along at a maximum speed of 255mph, the SBD had a tremendous range of over 1,000 miles and could carry over 2,000lb of bombs. To make its attack run, the Dauntless pilot would nose over into a 70-degree dive, increasing his accuracy and making him more difficult to hit by anti-aircraft gunners. He would then deploy dive flaps, with perforated flaps at the trailing edge of the wing to increase drag and control during the dive. The Dauntless would reach its top speed, and the pilot would release his bomb between 2,000 and 2,500ft above his target. Pulling out at about 900ft above the ground, the pilot would experience 4Gs, but in a high-threat area, the dive recovery might occur even lower to the ground, forcing the pilot to pull as much as 9Gs to recover.

Dauntless pilots left their indelible mark on history during the Battle of Midway, sinking four Japanese fleet carriers: *Akagi, Hiryu, Kaga,* and *Soryu,* effectively turning the tide of the war in the Pacific by inflicting losses so great that the Japanese could not replace the men and material.

The Dauntless earned its nickname of "Slow, But Deadly" (SBD) by giving the US Navy its first significant victory of the war and effectively changing naval doctrine, proving once and for all that battleships would no longer be the dominant force at sea, but rather the aircraft carrier would rule the waves from then on. Although outmatched in a dogfight, in the hands of the right pilot, the Dauntless could also defend itself against the more maneuverable Zero, and one such pilot was Lieutenant Stanley "Swede" Vejtasa. On May 7, 1942, Vejtasa was jumped by seven Zeros and was forced to fight for his life in a slow but rugged aircraft. Turning tightly and maneuvering erratically, he was able to score two kills with his .50cal machine guns, and this third victory occurred when he rammed a Zero, slicing off its wing tip. Eventually, the Dauntless was replaced by the Curtiss SB2C Helldiver, which was faster and had a greater range.

The Dixie Wing of the CAF has restored a remarkable Dauntless, named *Speedy D*, painted to reflect an SBD in service during the Marianas Turkey Shoot, and according to pilot Keith Wood, "It is authentic right down to the smallest details and is operational today, flying to roughly 20 airshows per year throughout the Southeast and Midwest." The original airframe was built in 1944 in El Segundo, California, and was most likely used to transport VIPs or other dignitaries, and, as a result, never saw action. It was struck from the inventory in 1947 and was sold to a skywriting company but was again sold when its fuel consumption was too great for its budget. It then flew for a Mexican aerial photography company in 1951, primarily surveying oil fields. In 1966, the Planes of Fame Museum bought the Dauntless and put it on display until the CAF bought it in

1971, and it stayed on display until the early 1990s until it was decided to fully restore it to flying status. It finally took to the air again in 1999. More of Dixie Wing's SBD history can be viewed at https://airbasegeorgia.org/douglas-sbd-5/.

Another famous Dauntless is Planes of Fame's *White 39*, which was originally constructed in 1943 and flew 30 combat missions with the Royal New Zealand Air Force. It then served with the US Navy and Marine Corps until it was sold to Warner Bros., where it starred in several movies including *Midway*. It was then sold to the Planes of Fame in 1959 and flew again in 1987. The history of *White 39* can be found at https://planesoffame.org/aircraft/plane-SBD-5.

ABOVE: Maneuvering in to show center, this Dauntless proves that, even as a bomber, it was still nimble and easy to handle.

LEFT: The Planes of Fame's SBD is equipped with a simulated bomb, drawing attention to its dive-bombing mission.

OPPOSITE: The dive flaps can be seen on the trailing edge of the wing, slowing the Dauntless down in a dive.

Getting ready for a simulated attack, this Dauntless lines up its target on the runway.

Flying away after a successful bomb run, the SBD has completed another mission.

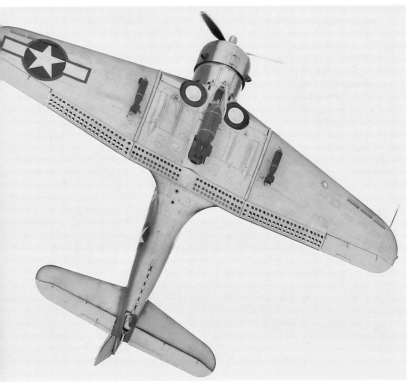

The CAF's Dauntless shows that it can also carry two smaller bombs on the wings, adding more lethality to the SBD.

The CAF gets every detail right, including the yellow stripes on the bombs that indicate they are active.

The FHCAM's beautifully restored Spitfire is a dream to fly and to photograph.

# CHAPTER 25
# SPITFIRE

Symbolizing British resolve, the Supermarine Spitfire stood up to a seemingly invincible Luftwaffe and beat them back decisively, ensuring that German boots would not tread on English soil. The high performance of the Spitfire made it incredibly popular with British citizens, as it successfully defended against the vaunted Bf 109 and helped stop the devastating bomber raids. Designed for maximum aerodynamic efficiency, the Spitfire utilized flush rivets for uninterrupted airflow, and the iconic elliptical wings that were thin enough to reduce drag but thick enough to house the landing gear and weapons. The Spitfire was fast, able to travel at 370mph, powered by the legendary Rolls Royce Merlin 45 engine, and packed a punch with its two 20mm cannons and four .303cal machine guns. Its main limitation was its short range, but it was designed specifically as a home defense interceptor to ward off incoming bombers, a mission at which it exceled. Over 20,000 Spitfires were built, making it the most produced Allied fighter of the war and the only Allied fighter in production throughout the entire conflict. It also served in the Pacific as the initial bulwark against Japanese aggression and although outmaneuvered by the Zero, it proved capable of slashing attacks and staved off immediate defeat. Many variants emerged, including the Seafire, which was capable of taking off from aircraft carriers, and the Mk.24, which chased down V-1 flying bombs.

While the Spitfire was undoubtedly the face of the Battle of Britain, it also participated in many other important battles, including blunting Italian air attacks on Malta, and serving with the Soviet Union on the Eastern Front. It also was a decent photo reconnaissance aircraft, and it replaced the Bristol Blenheim and Westland Lysander, which were too slow and lightly armed to effectively make their way to the target. Photo reconnaissance missions required a high level of skill for precision flying, making sure that the camera and aircraft were at the correct angles so that the target would be adequately photographed. One of the most notable reconnaissance missions undertaken by a Spitfire occurred after the famous Dam Busters Raid, when Bomber Command requested a damage assessment of the Dams struck during Operation *Chastise*. Flying Officer Frank Fray was the lone Spitfire pilot who provided photographic proof of the success of the raid, flying his mission on May 17, 1943, and successfully relaying pictures of the destruction. He also flew the same reconnaissance mission three days earlier, and Bomber Command was able to display the effectiveness of the bombing and use it to boost the morale of the British citizenry. Photo Spitfires also provided support for the D-Day invasion and Operation *Market Garden*. After the war, Spitfires continued to serve in low-intensity conflicts until they were replaced by jet-powered aircraft.

There are over 50 airworthy Spitfires worldwide, as their iconic status makes them a popular collector's item, and one such example is housed at the FHCAM. Its Spitfire, *ZDU*, is a combat veteran, flying with RAF No. 312 Squadron and piloted by Squadron Leader Tomas Vybiral. It was hit by flak, narrowly missing Vybiral, and, after repairs, it continued with the RAF until 1958, when it served as a gate guard for RAF Bridgnorth until 1964, when it was sold to the Air Museum of Calgary in Alberta. Later, it was sold to a private collector who attempted to restore it to airworthiness, but this was not completed, and it was shipped back to England to be completely refurbished. Finally, in 1999, the FHCAM acquired *ZDU*, and has flown it routinely alongside other restored RAF aircraft, including the Mosquito and Hurricane, in its Battle of Britain tribute. More information about the FHCAM's Spitfire can be found at http://flyingheritage.org/Explore/The-Collection/Britain/Supermarine-Spitfire-Mk-Vc.aspx.

**ABOVE:** Serving during the "finest hour," the Spitfire defended Britain from the Luftwaffe onslaught, giving the German pilots all they could handle in a dogfight.

**ABOVE RIGHT:** The elliptical wings gave additional aerodynamic qualities to the Spitfire while also providing wonderful aesthetics for aviation enthusiasts.

**RIGHT:** This Spitfire represents Squadron No. 312, a Czech unit, and highlights the resolve of the Czech pilots, who were willing to fight on even after their country had been conquered.

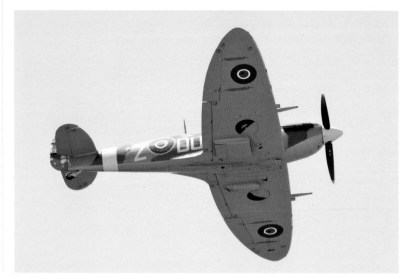

The Spitfire was beloved by pilots of all nationalities, often referred to as a "ballerina in the sky."

The Battle of Britain tribute from the FHCAM is always a sight to see, since these types are rare in the US.

*ZDU* is flanked by its larger counterparts, and the size difference between the Spitfire and the Mosquito and Thunderbolt is apparent in this photo.

*ZDU* escorts *TV959*; a similar flight may have occurred during World War Two.

The tailhook at the aft of the Avenger was supremely important in stopping this heavy beast during carrier landings.

# CHAPTER 26
# AVENGER

The most successful torpedo bomber of World War Two was the Grumman TBF Avenger, sinking the super battleships *Yamato* and *Musahi* and sinking at least 30 enemy submarines. It was also the heaviest single-engined aircraft during the war, with a maximum takeoff weight of nearly 18,000lb, a massive amount for any aircraft during that era, let alone a carrier-based bomber. Powered by a Wright R-2600 engine, the Avenger had 1,700hp, a maximum speed of 280mph, a range of 900 miles, and carried a 2,000lb Mark 13 torpedo in its bomb-bay. It also carried two .50cal machine guns in its wings and had two rear-facing machine guns for self-defense, with a .50cal gun on the dorsal side and a .30cal gun on the ventral side. Avengers carried a crew of three: a pilot, top turret gunner, and radioman/navigator/ventral gunner. Seemingly ungainly because of its massive size, it was reasonably maneuverable and easy to handle, proving useful as a command aircraft to direct the air battle. Its bulk and payload enabled it to carry large radars to take on anti-submarine and airborne early warning and control roles. While most of the exploits of the Avenger occurred in the Pacific, it played an important role during the Battle of the Atlantic, escorting convoys against roving U-boats. Nearly 10,000 Avengers were built and were used as experimental platforms by various air forces around the world, until the last one was retired in the 1960s.

During the Battle of Midway, the Avenger faced a tough baptism of fire, losing five out of six aircraft with the sixth one badly damaged and all crew members either wounded or killed. However, better tactics and improved pilot skill helped increase the lethality of the Avenger, and its redemption occurred during the Battle of Guadalcanal, where it helped sink the battleship *Hiei*. The most famous Avenger aviator was Lieutenant George H. W. Bush, who would later become the 41st US President. In September 1944, Bush was shot down in his Avenger during an attack on Chichi Jima's radio stations. He subsequently baled out and was eventually rescued by the submarine USS *Finback* and returned to his squadron eight weeks later. His other two crew members did not survive the bale out. Improvements in Japanese anti-aircraft accuracy and the slow speed of the Avenger made torpedo attacks more difficult and less effective, forcing the TBM to move to other roles such as close air support and cargo transport. Fortunately, the Avenger was well-suited to these roles because of its high payload capabilities. After the war, many Avengers were sold and converted to fire bombers, able to drop 600 gallons of fire retardant.

Grumman was the initial manufacturer of the Avenger, and its aircraft were labeled as TBF, but their capacity was limited, so, under license, General Motors also built most of the almost 10,000 Avengers, designated as TBM. The Planes of Fame Museum has a wonderfully restored TBM-3E, which was originally built in 1945, slated to serve on board the USS *Franklin* but the aircraft carrier never returned to sea or combat, and the aircraft was placed in surplus. It was sold to the Planes of Fame in 1958 and restored to airworthiness in 1976. Because the Avenger was designed to carry a crew of three, the Planes of Fame offers passenger rides in exchange for donations to help keep the museum running, which is an awesome opportunity to support living history while having a once-in-a-lifetime experience of flying in an acclaimed warbird. More information about the Avenger can be found at https://planesoffame.org/aircraft/plane-TBM-3E.

**ABOVE LEFT:** This belly view of the Avenger shows the ventral turret and the large torpedo bay.

**ABOVE RIGHT:** Nimble for such a large and heavy aircraft, the Avenger was able to maneuver into position, avoiding as much anti-aircraft fire as possible.

**LEFT:** The rear gunners made sure that the Avenger's tail was clear during its attack run.

**OPPOSITE:** Escorted by a Wildcat, this Avenger relied on fighter support to chase enemy fighters away during its torpedo run.

Spitfire *ZDU* is flanked by Hurricane *Z5429* and Mosquito *TV959*.

# EPILOGUE

World War Two changed the way wars are fought by introducing air combat as an equal battlefield to the land and sea, not just simply a supporting role. The machines that flew into the fight had to be tough to withstand enemy fire, and the men who piloted them had to be even tougher, because much of what they were asked to do was experimental and untested in the real world. To pay tribute to these heroes, wonderful and dedicated volunteers around the country have contributed their time and money to restore these aircraft to their former glory. Although nothing can truly repay the World War Two veterans who fought and died for their countries, flying their old aircraft again keeps their memories alive and helps future generations to stay invested in their histories. As the number of World War Two veterans sadly dwindles, it becomes even more important to support these organizations who do their part to pay back the debt of gratitude owed to these heroes.

*Tallahassee Lassie* taxis out to the runway at FHCAM, with its 12 aerial victories on display beneath the cockpit.

# FURTHER READING

Bilstein, R. E., *Airlift and Airborne Operations in World War II,* Air Force History and Museums Program (1998)

Byrd, M., *Chennault: Giving Wings to the Tiger*, University of Alabama Press (2003)

Douglas, S., and Wright, R., *Combat and Command; the Story of an Airman in Two World Wars*, Simon and Schuster (1966)

Douhet, G., *The Command of the Air*, Office of Air Force History (1983)

Honeycutt, T. D., *Cram's Rams: A History of Marine Bombing Squadron Six-Twelve in World War II* (1989)

Horne, John E., "Douglas B-26s in Korea," *Air Enthusiast*, Number 24, Pilot Press, 1984, pp. 50–59.

Mets, D. R., *Master of Airpower: General Carl A. Spaatz*, Presidio Press (1997)

Mitchell, W., *Winged Defense: The Development and Possibilities of Modern Air Power*, University of Alabama Press (2009)

Sakai, S., *Samurai!*, Bantam (1985)

Unruh, A. B., *The Shadow Casters: My Journey through War*. Pegasus Imaging Co. (1999)